ACTS:
AN INDUCTIVE STUDY

ACTS:
AN INDUCTIVE STUDY

A Manual on
Bible-Study-in-Depth

By
IRVING L. JENSEN

MOODY PRESS • Chicago

ACKNOWLEDGMENTS

The map of the Roman world (p. 8) is adapted from the map *New Testament World* by permission of American Bible Society, New York. Drawings of ground plan and structure of Herod's Temple (p. 87) are reproduced from *The New Bible Dictionary,* by permission of Inter-Varsity Fellowship, London.

Second Printing, 1970

Library of Congress Catalog Card Number: 67-14390

Printed in the United States of America

CONTENTS

38785

PREFACE

ACTS is the church's standard textbook on the first three decades of its history and its ageless global task of evangelization. The Bible student of this generation has the unique privilege of viewing the church from two opposite vantage points—that of the church's beginnings, as narrated in Acts, and that of its end times, as recorded by the daily newspaper. Any alert Christian cannot but be concerned over the comparisons he is compelled to make.

Acts has inspired many excellent commentaries. This study manual is not another commentary but a guide to the personal, inductive study of Acts. Its main purpose is to help the reader train his eyes to see for himself what Luke wrote and how he wrote it. By capturing insights into the miracle of the first century church it is hoped that the reader will involve himself more personally in the mission of the twentieth century church.

The use of a triad—the Bible, the reader's eyes and a pencil—which is discussed in this manual's companion, *Independent Bible Study,* is a simple but proven formula of fruitful Bible study for any earnest Christian. Therefore, a constant appeal is made in the manual to record observations on paper. Not only should the analytical chart be used to record one's studies, but the reader also is encouraged throughout the manual to adapt the other methods. Ultimately the spiritual fruit produced will be evident as the Holy Spirit causes the student's heart to burn even as did the hearts of Christ's disciples (Luke 24:32).

The author recognizes with deep gratitude the incentive his wife has been to him as well as her countless hours of secretarial assistance in this project.

IRVING L. JENSEN

7

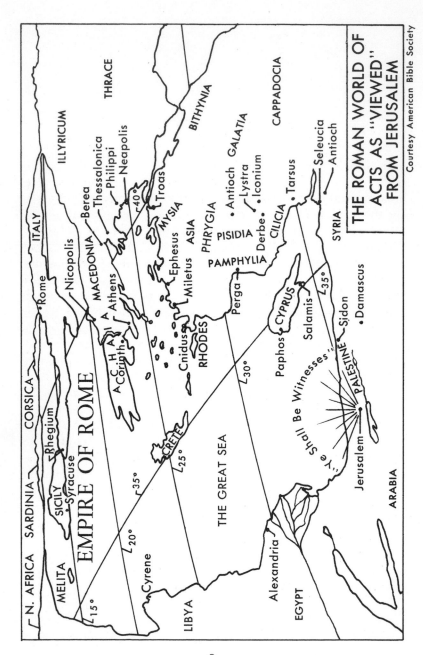

THE ROMAN WORLD OF
ACTS AS "VIEWED"
FROM JERUSALEM

Courtesy American Bible Society

8

Part One

ORIENTATION

"There is a great harvest," he told them,
"but only a few are working in it
   —which means
      you must pray to the Lord of the harvest
      that he will send out more reapers."

LUKE 10:2 (PHILLIPS)

CHAPTER ONE

INTRODUCTION

THE SEQUEL to any momentous event may be as significant as the event itself. Compare for instance the Hiroshima bomb and the subsequent peace treaty with Japan; the Wall Street crash of 1929 and the depression that followed; the invention of the printing press and the later Bible distribution; the consecration of William Carey and the cause of modern missions.

Acts is clearly the sequel to the Gospels; its story of the church is the wonderful continuation of the unique and fantastic story of Christ's earthly life. Beyond this, Acts provides the key for the fuller understanding of the Epistles which follow Acts in the New Testament canon and interpret the gospel which Christ lived and preached.

Consider for a few moments the core of the Gospels' history: Jesus came from heaven and then returned to heaven, accomplishing His Father's will while He was here on earth. This was His time-bound, eternity-affecting life. The Gospels tell the story of that wonderful life, but only a few pages relate the events of the few weeks of his post-resurrection ministry. The Bible's history would conclude with an abrupt void if the account of what the resurrected Christ did to men's hearts was limited to only a few instances, such as the two men's reaction, "Did not our hearts burn within us while he talked with us?" and Thomas', "My Lord and my God!" Acts was designed by God to complete the story of the Gospels, by showing the gospel of the resurrected Christ at work, transforming men's hearts and making them witnesses of the Way, through the ministry of the Holy Spirit sent to earth for that purpose. This is illustrated by the accompanying chart:

11

RELATION OF ACTS TO THE GOSPELS

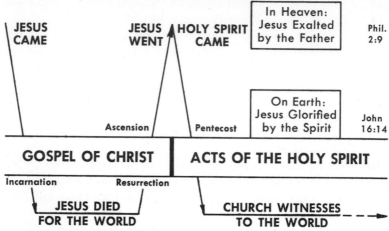

So, Christ's death and resurrection were crucial for mankind, for there would be no gospel without them. And as they bring about the effective working of the gospel in men's hearts, there also may be assigned to that working the importance of proof that they were efficacious—as Christ said.

In Acts Luke has brought together a world-shaking story of the first thirty years of the Christian church. It is a book of color and action written by an artist who uses words which are wholly accurate and vital as to fact and exhortation. Miracles abound, and supernatural power energizes the children of God. It is a book about people—good and bad—and their reactions to truth and righteousness. Its heroes demonstrate courage and endurance, compassion for human hearts and devotion to an eternal cause. The book exposes the sins and weaknesses of men and the wiles of the devil and his servants. On its pages are clearly written the simplicity of the gospel, the mystery of God's grace and the sureness of judgment for sin. For life, there are patterns to follow and sins to avoid. It is a book about individual men and women, the church and missions. It demonstrates the existence of Christ and assures His second coming. Putting priority on eternal, spiritual truths, it shows the relative smallness of all else. The flag of the Christian gospel waves high throughout, never giving

way to the white flag of surrender. Acts begins with the triumphant voice of the resurrected Christ and ends with the unhindered
preaching of one of His noble servants.

Acts was not written to furnish a system of doctrine for the
church, nor even to do much interpreting of the tremendous truths
of the gospel. This task was assigned by the Spirit of God to those
later inspired to write the Epistles. Acts reports the gospel in action, and it is the Christian student's opportunity—a wonderful and
challenging one—to seek out the universal timeless principles sup-
ported by those historical facts, by which Christians and the
church may live and serve God. The "tongues as of fire" on Pentecost Day were not to be a normative occurrence for Christians,
but they teach a principle which the student of Acts should discover. The death stroke upon Ananias and Sapphira for their
lying was not intended to teach similar death for all subsequent
lying, but it dramatically illustrated a timeless principle.

So here is your starting point as you open the pages of Acts to
learn its message. Acts was written for *you*, and the challenge
could not be more personal. Notice Luke's first words: "The first
account I composed, Theophilus, about all that Jesus began to do
and teach. . . ." Luke was writing with a specific man, Theophilus,
in mind. Theophilus was a personal acquaintance of Luke[1] and
Luke wrote him a story that was both real and pertinent to the
life of the man and to the world in which he lived. In no lesser
degree is Acts intended personally for you, being as it is a part of
God's inspired Book written to all the world. All this makes you
not only the student but also the object of the Book's spiritual
purposes.

Personal, inductive Bible study is a live challenge. What the
Bible says, you must see; and what it means, you must learn.
Study that is superficial or casual will overlook the golden nuggets. Study that unduly magnifies the technical minutiae and
neglects the large ideas and movements will induce a haze of ob-
scure and impractical notions. Study-in-depth, which is the object
of this study manual, avoids those superficial and technical ap-

---

[1]Some feel that the name Theophilus is fictitious, intended by Luke to
represent all who would subsequently read the book. This appears to be an
unnatural interpretation.

proaches that are extreme, and engages rather in a practical, sound, comprehensive and objective firsthand analysis of the Word.

Consider the zeal and curiosity of Paul's Berean audience, who "accepted the message most eagerly and studied the scriptures every day to see . . ." (Acts 17:11, Phillips Translation). Your progress in studying Acts will depend much on your own personal desire, zeal and initiative to know what God has said in this book by Luke.

Chapter Two

PURPOSES OF THE MANUAL

This book on the inductive study of Acts is primarily a manual intended to assist in private firsthand study of the text of Acts. The book is also a companion volume to the author's work *Independent Bible Study*,[1] in which a description of the analytical-inductive-chart method of Bible study is presented.

This manual on Acts will not do the studying for you. The questions of each lesson are designed to lead you to the Spirit's intention of the biblical text under observation. Help is given along the way, but it will not inhibit your own independent study. The main purpose of the manual is to provide guidance and incentive. All in all, by following its procedures you should be able to develop strong and desirable habits of original Bible study, the acme of personal Bible study. Beyond this, your involvement in recording your observations on the analytical charts will develop your ability to communicate to others for the simple reason that you are continually organizing and recasting the biblical text, expressing it in your own way in clear and understandable outline form. This communication aspect of Bible-study-in-depth is an appropriate conclusion to the study process, the four steps being: observation (What does it say?), interpretation (What does it mean?), application (How does it apply today?), and communication (How may I give this to others?).

As noted above, the inductive method of study underlies all your steps and procedures as you undertake this study of Acts. The method is both nontechnical and natural in its approach to the biblical text, on the basis that the Bible was not written primarily for the professional scholar but for Everyman. Some of the

[1]Chicago: Moody Press, 1963.

more prominent characteristics of the inductive method may be summarized as follows:

1) letting the Bible text speak for itself
2) observation first; then interpretation and application
3) analysis of what the Bible says (content), and how it says it (form or structure); a study-in-depth
4) awareness of explicit and implied truths
5) original, firsthand study predominant

Your study of Acts by this inductive method should prove not only objectively accurate, but personally wholesome.

The manual has been prepared so as to be equally profitable for individual Bible study, group study and the classroom situation. For group study, each member should do the analysis of each lesson before meeting time; then the various analyses may be compared and observations shared when the group meets. The interesting feature of this method of study is that no two analyses will be alike. In the classroom situation the student's analysis is the core of the homework assignment. He should be encouraged to develop an eye for observation and the facility of expressing his discoveries in an organized manner on the analytical chart. In the analyses the teacher will have a visual and measurable check on the progress of the student in his learning how to study the Bible for himself.

The main purposes of the study manual are to serve as a guide, a help and an incentive. You should be aware of these purposes in order to use the manual most profitably.

I. AS A GUIDE

Throughout the manual suggestions will appear concerning what to look for in the text of Acts. The observations themselves will be yours. Beyond this, the ultimate goal to strive for in this phase of Bible study is to be able to personally determine those paths of inquiry. In practice, knowing what to look for and then finding it are so intimately related that experience in the latter automatically gives training in the former. The types of questions posed throughout the lessons usually cannot be answered merely by listing facts. In the observation process of study it is true that such mere facts must be observed, but the ultimate purpose is to discover the significance of the facts.[2] The author has attempted to use a variety of types of questions, all of which are aimed at something deeper than the facts per se. It will help the reader to become acquainted with the following types of questions in order to appreciate more fully what he has been asked to find:

A. *Projection Question*

This asks you to visualize the setting and action in order to realize the pertinence and significance of any related questions. In this you are projecting yourself. An example of this question would be: "If you were Barnabas, what thoughts would be running through your mind at this time?"

B. *Composition Question*

Here you try to determine why Luke recorded an item in the manner he did, to learn the intended emphasis of a spiritual truth.

C. *Implication Question*

This question prompts you to seek the subsurface, not-so-obvious truth underlying the record. This is sometimes the richest nugget in the Word.

D. *Motivation Question.*

You are asked why the biblical characters acted as they did, and how you evaluate that action.

E. *Transposition Question*

Here you are transposing the action into the present day. Such a question might read, "How would Paul have planned his evangelistic crusades in a country of this twentieth century?" This is a type of application question.

F. *Context Question*

Because the Bible is its best interpreter, this type of question appears repeatedly throughout the manual. The student is direc-

[2]An example of a mere factual question might be, "How many apostles were there when Matthias was added to the number?" (1:26). A more important question, searching for the significance aspect, would be, "Why twelve—no more and no less?"

ted not so much to distant cross-references (a valuable study in itself) as to the immediate context.

G. *Application Question*

This asks for the derivation of a spiritual application from the text, the desired end of all Bible study.

Besides helping you discover treasures in the book of Acts, this manual is intended to guide you in developing fruitful and efficient study methods and recording procedures for the study of any book of the Bible. You should feel free to adapt and alter any mechanical or nonmechanical procedures suggested; it is obvious that flexibility will be an asset.

As indicated earlier, Bible study groups will be helped in various ways by the manual. For example, the teacher, who is expected to do more than the class members, may choose to duplicate at least a condensed version of his analytical chart on a blackboard, teaching as he records. Each class member will want to do his own analytical chart, comparing studies during the class session. The practical questions of each lesson will serve as starters for discussion sessions.

II. AS A HELP[3]

Considering the vast scope and depth of its contents, the Bible is remarkably perspicuous, which minimizes the need for outside aids to its study. Of course, the more technical the study of the biblical text is, the more the helps are needed. The section entitled EXPLANATIONS in each lesson is included to answer questions about terms in the biblical passage which the context does not afford. Light thus shed on the difficult terms (sometimes made so because of history or geography) leaves the student free to concentrate his attention on the analytical aspect of his study.

Chapter 4 (of Part One) of this manual outlines the major elements of the large background to Acts, while similar notes are included in the study lessons. Historical tables, maps and charts also serve this function. (Due to limitations of space, the amount of background help in this manual has been kept to a minimum.)

[3]A description of the manual as a study tool, with respect to the lesson areas, is given in chapter 3.

Finally, this manual suggests various volumes for reference for the reader interested in doing further research in Acts.

III. AS AN INCENTIVE

Your first desire and impulse to study Acts should never be allowed to dampen or grow cold. Instead, your interest in what Luke has to say through inspiration of the Holy Spirit should be nurtured and intensified. This manual is to serve as an incentive in this direction. If it can prevent you from becoming bogged down in any difficult portion or from easing off in the familiar, if it can sharpen your eyes to see more and more from lesson to lesson, and if it can stir in your heart the need for your own life to be quickened by Acts' message, then it will have served this purpose.

Chapter Three

STUDY TOOLS

An analytical study of a biblical passage differs from a devotional reading in that it demands a minimum of tools for the construction. Just as good tools are vital for a good carpenter, so good tools are essential for fruitful analytical Bible study. There are the materials (tangible tools), and there is the approach (intangible), the latter being just as much a set of tools as the former. Each is discussed below.

I. THE MATERIALS

A. *A Study Bible*

The Bible in your mother tongue—English—is the basic text for personal study. For analysis, the English New Testament text should be an accurate representation of the original Greek text, and it should not be a free paraphrase. The *New American Standard Bible: New Testament (Reference Edition)*[1] is a highly recommended translation of the New Testament fulfilling such requirements. This version is a revision of the New Testament of the *American Standard Version* (1901),[2] retaining most of the advantages of the latter while offering many more. Unfortunately the paragraph format of the *American Standard Version* is dropped, but this is compensated by a functional one-column text and by

---

[1]This version was produced under the auspices of the Lockman Foundation, sponsor of the Amplified Bible. It is published by the Foundation Press, and marketed by three co-publishers: Broadman Press, Moody Press and World Publishing Company (1963). The text edition of this version appeared in 1965, without cross-references or marginal notes. The reference edition is the one recommended by this manual.

[2]New York: Thomas Nelson & Sons. Throughout this manual the abbreviations NASB and ASV refer to the *New American Standard Bible* and *American Standard Version*, respectively.

shorter paragraph[3] units. Unless otherwise specified, all references in this manual to the New Testament text are from this *New American Standard Bible (Reference Edition)*. Quotations of the Old Testament text are from the *American Standard Version*.

If the *American Standard Version* is used for this inductive study of Acts, it is advisable for the student to use an edition that facilitates analytical study. Two editions that so qualify are a large study edition of the entire Bible published by Thomas Nelson and Sons, and a loose-leaf edition of only the New Testament published by the American Bible Society. The former is valuable for its cross-references, the latter for its wide margins for notations.

If the reader should prefer to use the *King James Version* as his basic study text, the major purposes and benefits of this manual will still apply.

B. *Other Bible Versions*

The value of modern Bible versions for study purposes is mainly in (1) the comparative study of phrases and (2) the recognition of the flowing connected movement of the biblical passages. One free rendering (e.g., Phillips)[4] and one expanded translation (e.g., Wuest)[5] should serve your study purposes well. However, most of your time and concentration should be in the basic study text.

C. *Writing Materials*

"Jot it down" is the byword here. For your analytical studies you should be equipped with the following:

paper: 8½″×11″ (unruled; good quality)

pens: blue, black, red ink (fine-line ball-point pens recommended)

pencils: a set of colored pencils

ruler: 12″

There are many advantages to writing out your studies, but only three are mentioned here. First, your eye to observe is developed, for you must see before you can record. Second, record-

---

[3]The "paragraph" units are indicated by bold-face verse numbers.
[4]J. B. Phillips, *New Testament in Modern English* (New York: The Macmillan Co., 1958). This translation is available in a paperback edition.
[5]Kenneth S. Wuest, *The New Testament: An Expanded Translation* (Grand Rapids: Wm. B. Eerdmans Publishing Co., 1961).

ing your observations on an analytical chart helps you to study
methodically, organizing your findings. Third, whatever you record becomes your permanent possession, a boon also to the short
memory.

D. *Commentaries and Other Helps*

The tendency of the average Bible student is to lean too heavily
and prematurely on available commentaries and other outside
aids. The thrill of firsthand discovery is thus forfeited, and the
student's self-confidence and independent study are weakened.
Extra-biblical aids obviously are valuable, but they must be used
to enhance rather than hinder independent study. The rule of
thumb is to refer to such aids only after one has analyzed the
Bible passage. There are exceptions. For example, if your original
analysis depends on the explanation of a problem passage, you
may choose to seek outside help. First, however, see if the problem can be solved from the context; you will be surprised how
often the context is sufficient commentary!

Three valuable outside aids for Bible study are a commentary,
a Bible dictionary and an exhaustive concordance. In recent years
very excellent one-volume commentaries and dictionaries have
been published, enhancing the toolbox of the Bible student.

These lessons are geared to study Acts with a minimal use of
outside aids. The student who desires to make a more advanced
study of any particular subject will need to refer to the technical
aids.

E. *The Manual as a Tool*

In a real sense this manual is a study tool. Each lesson has six
sections which are intended to help you in your study of Acts as
shown below:

1) *Introduction.* Primarily the introduction serves to relate the
present lesson to the previous one and to furnish any background
material pertinent to the study.

2) *Preparation for study.* Empathy is a key to an effective approach to a Bible passage. In order to help you project yourself
into the situation of the passage, various suggestions are offered.

Use your controlled imagination to advantage here. Brief studies also are presented in this section for your consideration preliminary to the analysis project.

3) *Analysis.* This is the heart of your study. The two processes are *observe* and *record.* Suggestions are offered in this section on what to look for; the analytical chart is one place to record your *organized* findings. Suggestions for applying the biblical truths are also found in this section.

4) *Explanations.* A minimum of background help is given here. Study questions also appear occasionally. You may choose to read this section before you proceed with your analysis.

5) *Further advanced study.* Extra studies are offered in this section on an optional basis. The continuity of the manual's lessons is not dependent on the completion of these studies.

6) *Words to ponder.* As a concluding exercise, ponder the weight of the biblical words quoted here. Apply them to your own circumstances. If possible, write a paragraph or two on a theme suggested by the words.

II. THE APPROACH

How you approach the Scriptures in study has much to do with what your study produces. Both your spiritual approach and mental approach must be healthy and right.

A. *Spiritual Approach*

First, you must have a faith in God who gave the Word you are studying: (1) that His inspiration of the original writers brought forth only infallible words; (2) that His preservation of the Scriptures through the centuries guarantees a substantially pure text today; (3) that His recorded truths are unchangeable and indestructible ("The grass withereth, the flower fadeth; but the word of our God shall stand forever" Isa. 40:8).

Second, you must depend on the Holy Spirit for understanding the truths you are reading. This is the grand dependency within the discipline of independent, inductive Bible study.

Third, you must actively engage your heart to seek the counsel of God and to be moved by His Spirit, that you may walk thereby.

A sensitive spirit to the Spirit's sensitive Word is the setting for a work of God in the heart.

B. *Mental Approach*

The mind with all its amazing facilities is a creation of God, and the mind at work in the study of the Bible is a holy engagement. It is inconsistent for a Christian to be meticulous in his business affairs but slovenly in Bible study. Effective Bible study demands a mental approach that is as alert, active, eager, open to new vistas, discerning, thorough and humble as is possible for the student. One of the main emphases urged by the analytical method is to tarry over the biblical text, availing oneself of the waiting benefits which accrue to him who would hear. At the same time an extreme passivity with no diligent inquiring activity is to be avoided. Another intangible study tool which the student should use is that of methodical study. Haphazardness in Bible study is not only unproductive, it is often misleading. Methodical study gives high priority to the search for related things in the Bible passage, for the awareness of context is perhaps the best single aid to interpretation.

Three wonderful facts justify serious personal Bible study:
1) God gave the Bible
2) The Bible waits to be studied diligently
3) God gives what is necessary to study the Bible.

An unstudied Bible in the hands of a Christian is a symptom of spiritual blight. The healthy Christian continually prays from his heart, as did the psalmist, "Teach me thy statutes" (Ps. 119:68b). This should be your basic spiritual and mental approach to your study of Acts.

Chapter Four

THE WORLD OF THE EARLY CHURCH

THE BOOK OF ACTS and the reason for its existence assume added significance when we begin to comprehend the world in which the early believers lived—the world of unevangelized souls which would be the parish of the disciples so recently commissioned by their Lord.

Jesus commanded this handful of disciples in Jerusalem to reach beyond the horizon to the peoples of the uttermost lands in order to make them disciples also. Could such a task be accomplished? What were the problems? Who were the foes? How could they communicate? Need the message be adapted to the differing backgrounds? Upon what secular helps and advantages could the church depend? The answers to these and other related questions are enhanced by the facts of the historical, cultural and religious backgrounds of the years of the early church.

Due to limitations of space in this manual, it is not possible to treat these backgrounds in detail. You are encouraged to do reading in this area in outside sources.[1] The following outline will serve to suggest topics which should be the object of your research.

I. GEOGRAPHY OF THE ROMAN EMPIRE

A. Study the map on page 8, *The Roman World of Acts as Viewed from Jerusalem.* Try to visualize the apostles' concept of

[1]For example, see the following: Merrill C. Tenney, *New Testament Survey*, rev. ed. (Grand Rapids: Wm. B. Eerdmans Publishing Co., 1961), pp. 1-120; Richard B. Rackham, *The Acts of the Apostles* (13th ed.; London: Methuen & Co. Ltd., 1947), pp. lv-lxi; cxii-cxv; F. F. Bruce, *The Acts of the Apostles* (Chicago: Inter-Varsity Press, 1952), pp. 55-58; O. T. Manley (ed.), *The New Bible Handbook* (Chicago: Inter-Varsity Press, 1963), pp. 276-97; Erich Sauer, *The Dawn of World Redemption* (Grand Rapids: Wm. Eerdmans Publishing Co., 1953), pp. 265-86.

the vastness of their task. Consult other books for a description of
the Roman Empire's lands and waters.

B. Christianity spread in all directions from Jerusalem after
Christ's ascension. Why do you think Acts records only the westward advance?[2]

II. THE CULTURAL ENVIRONMENT

Three major forces (combinations of such things as culture,
religion, knowledge and tradition) affected the environment which
formed the life and makeup of the peoples described in Acts.
Those three forces were the Jewish, Greek and Roman elements.

Judaism was one important element of the culture. Negatively,
it was known for its false sects, its hard and impenetrable tradi-
tions, its rejection of Jesus as the Messiah and its zealous patriot-
ism. Positively, it stood for a belief in one God, the Old Testament Scriptures as the revelation of God, a search for salvation,
the salting influence of a believing remnant, a sense of destiny
and a faithful attendance at the worship services of the temple in
Jerusalem and the synagogues scattered throughout the empire.

Hellenism was another ingredient which vitally affected the
environment. Among its major contributions were a philosophical
spirit of inquiry that invaded its many religions, an attractive culture that sought the good and the beautiful, and, above all, its
vernacular koine Greek language, the universal medium of the
Roman world by which the gospel was communicated quickly
and efficiently.

The *Roman Empire* gave the church political and governmental
advantages. It guaranteed law and justice in hostile situations,
it provided roads, bridges and seaways for travel and it promoted
an underlying religious tolerance of the new religion of Christianity.

[2]For a history of the expansion of Christianity in the other directions, see
church history volumes such as Kenneth Scott Latourette, *A History of the
Expansion of Christianity,* Vol. I (New York: Harper & Bros., 1937), I, 86-
113. Latourette cites one tradition that arose in the early centuries of the
church concerning missionary work beyond Roman frontiers: "Sometimes in
the early centuries of Christianity the tradition arose that the Twelve Apostles had parcelled among themselves the known world. One form of this
tradition declared that Thomas received the Parthians as his assignment;
Matthew, Ethiopia; and Bartholomew, part of India" (p. 101).

It is highly recommended that you study these forces further, considering their component parts as you read.

Judaism:
> the Jews' history up to A.D. 30 (theocracy, persecution, dispersion)
> synagogue,[3] priesthood, scribes, elders, Sanhedrin
> covenant, Scriptures, Messianic hope, monotheism, temple, Holy City
> Jewish character, home, education
> sects: Pharisees, Sadducees, Essenes, Zealots

Hellenism:
> conquests of Alexander the Great (336-323 B.C.)
> Greek koine (common) language
> art, literature, education
> philosophies: Socrates, Plato, Aristotle, Epicurus, Zeno
> mystery religions

Roman Empire:
> organization: emperor, province, governor, proconsul, procurator
> Pax Romana (Roman Peace)
> roads, bridges, seaways
> religious tolerance, secularism

In addition to all the elements which made the environmental setting conducive to the gospel's propagation, there was the fact that the souls of the people needed an experience with Jesus—they needed spiritual rebirth. Since the hosts of religions and cults had offered nothing but disillusionment, it was truly the fullness of time for them to hear about Jesus (Gal. 4:4).

The apostles of Acts usually knew the audience to which they directed their evangel message, and spoke accordingly. They spoke most frequently to Jews, but sometimes their audience was predominantly heathen (e.g., Paul's message on Mars Hill, Acts 17).

---

[3]Jews were found in most of the cities of the empire, and Paul usually went to their synagogues on his arrival in a new city. Sauer has written, "Without the simple synagogue or the Jewish place of prayer (*proseuche*, Acts 16:13), the evangelistic activity of the apostle is scarcely conceivable" (*Op. cit.*, p. 179).

But they were always making the gospel relevant to all groups
as they taught divine authority and revelation, atonement by
Christ, salvation by grace through faith, fellowship with God and
a resurrection hope. Such a message made people either hungry
or mad; Acts was written to record their reactions.

CHAPTER FIVE

THE WRITING OF ACTS[1]

IT IS POSSIBLE to profitably study the text of the book of Acts without first being acquainted with the background of its history and environment and the story of its actual composition. But it is much more profitable first to learn the background of Acts and then, in the feel and spirit of its birth and being, to move along its streets and among its peoples, and thus to intimately learn its message. This chapter will acquaint you with Luke the man, why he wrote and how he wrote. Forget that he lived two thousand years ago, and dissolve all thoughts that men like Luke or Paul were supermen. They were men of human birth and passions who turned to Christ, learned of Him and served Him. Why not determine in your personal study of Acts to learn to be a servant like them?

I. THE AUTHOR

Most authorities agree that Luke was the writer of Acts. Extant ancient witnesses, dating as early as A.D. 170, are practically unanimous about this. The strongest internal evidence for Lucan authorship is the fact that Acts and the third gospel are both addressed to Theophilus, and Acts refers to a "former treatise" which obviously was the gospel. (Compare Luke 1:1-4 and Acts 1:1-5.)

Other internal evidences include (1) the similar style and language of the two writings; (2) the natural connection between the ending of the gospel and the beginning of Acts; (3) similarities such as the prominent place of women in both narratives. Further, the writer of Acts accompanied Paul on many of his

---

[1]Various titles were ascribed to Luke's book in the early days of its circulation. The three most common ones were "Acts of the Apostles" (found in the *Muratorian Fragment* on the Canon, of the late second century); "Acts of Apostles" (fourth century *Vaticanus* and *Beza* manuscripts); and "Acts" (fourth century *Sinaiticus* manuscript).

travels (as the "we" sections of Acts reveals: 16:10-17; 20:5–
21:18; 27:1–28:16),[2] and of the number of close associates of
Paul, Luke is most clearly identified as that fellow-traveler.[3]

A. Luke's Biography

Very little is known of Luke's life. Piecing together bits of information from here and there,[4] the story of his life might be described thus:

Luke was born of Greek parents, either in Antioch of Syria or
Philippi of Macedonia. The year of his birth was about the time
of the birth of Christ and also of Paul. He was named Lucas, a
shortened form of the Roman name Lucanus. Included in his
family was a brother Titus, who also was destined to be one of
Paul's fellow-laborers of the gospel.[5] Luke was kind, joyful, bright
and pious by nature. His university education was probably pur-
sued at Athens or Tarsus, where the curriculum would have afforded him training in philosophical thought and creative expression. His artistry with words was no doubt a native gift, but he
had good opportunity to develop it during these years of formal
study. Luke studied medical arts (Col. 4:14), a profession that
ranked high among the Greeks.

But Luke had yet to find God's purpose for Him. In fact, he
had yet to find God. Being a pious man, he sought to know God
and was very likely attracted to the local synagogue where he
listened to the Jews speak about their personal Jehovah. It was
at one of those synagogue services that he met Paul, who soon
led him to Christ and began taking him on his missionary ven-
tures. From time to time on his evangelistic tours Paul left Luke
behind to strengthen and organize the new band of converts in
a particular city; later Luke would rejoin Paul on the road.

[2]Luke no doubt was also with Paul at other times in the book of Acts,
even when Luke uses the third person in the narrative. Richard B. Rackham,
The Acts of the Apostles (13th ed.; London: Methuen & Co., Ltd., 1947),
p. xxvii.
[3]See Rackham, *op. cit.,* p. xvi, for evidences of this identification.
[4]The only places in the New Testament where the name Luke appears are
Colossians 4:14; II Timothy 4:11; Philemon 24. Any reconstruction of his
life is made mainly from implied or suggested facts, biblical or extrabiblical,
which are adequate for at least a general picture of his life.
[5]This fraternal relationship of Luke to Titus is only conjecture; such a relationship would account for the absence of Titus' name from Luke's narrative despite the fact that Titus was an important member of Paul's team.

During those precious years of experience as the beloved physician and attendant of Paul, he continually observed with keen eye, perhaps jotting down the experiences in a notebook and storing them in his memory for a later day. He was already being moved by the Holy Ghost to prepare for writing the early history of the church.

Luke, who never married, remained with Paul until Paul's death in A.D. 68 (cf. II Tim. 4:11). About fifteen years later, "at the age of eighty-four he fell asleep in Boeotia, full of the Holy Spirit."[6]

B. *Luke's Character*

More is revealed in the New Testament about Luke's character than about his life. To the extent that the personality of a biblical author is reflected in any divinely inspired writing, much about Luke is revealed in the content and style of his writing. As you proceed in your study of Acts, more and more of these traits will appear. Luke's personality traits show up in his relations with God and with men. He had a keen sense of the might, justice and holiness of God, with whom sin cannot dwell. Luke was a man of prayer who knew intimately the tonic of praise and the might of intercession. This will be evident as one studies the prayers in Acts. A joyful believer, Luke attached his heart whenever he reported an occasion of joy which resulted from the goodness and blessings of God.

Luke's relation to others was pure and vital too. His enthusiasm and devotion as a servant to his master Paul was consistent to the end. From Acts we observe his boundless love and sympathy for others in their needs. He had a gentle nature which sought to recognize persons who often were kept in the background. He was humble and self-effacing, giving himself no place in the narrative, but always exalting the other man.

As you study Acts, keep in mind the man whom God used to give you that text. In your study you will learn from the events of Acts, the people of Acts and the God of Acts. May you also learn from the writer of Acts!

[6]Quoted from the anti-Marcionite Prologue to Luke, c. A.D. 170.

II. DATE

Luke probably wrote Acts while in Rome toward the end of Paul's two-year imprisonment there, or about A.D. 61. He could not have completed his writing earlier than that, since Acts records that imprisonment (Acts 28:30), which is dated around A.D. 59-61. That he did not write Acts at a late date is obvious from the following:

1) The Jewish War of A.D. 66-70, climaxing in the holocaust of the destruction of Jerusalem (A.D. 70), is not even alluded to.

2) Nero's antichristian policy, following the great fire of Rome (A.D. 64), finds no place in the account.

3) Though Paul was in prison at the close of Acts, there is no suggestion in the narrative that Paul's death was imminent. Very likely Paul was soon released. After traveling about for a few years in evangelistic work even as far as Spain, Paul probably was arrested again and placed in the execution cell at Rome where he wrote his "dying letter," II Timothy, and then was finally executed shortly before Nero's suicide on June 8, A.D. 68.

III. SOURCES OF INFORMATION

Luke the master writer was also the master researcher. For his gospel he needed to interview many witnesses for their firsthand accounts of the life of Jesus. Research of oral and written sources also was required for Acts, but he had personally seen and heard much of its history or had learned about it from his intimate companion Paul. The accompanying chart shows the most probable sources of information for Luke's Acts.

NOTE:

1) Luke personally observed much, as is indicated by the three "we" sections. Also it should be noted that Luke may have witnessed the action of portions of Acts where he does *not* use "we" in his narrative. This may have been true regarding the large section of Acts 20:5 to 28:31.

2) Luke's main informant was Paul, who was able to supply not only the events of his conversion and missionary ministry but also other facts of the early church's history, such as Stephen's message and martyrdom (chapters 6-7).

OUTLINE OF ACTS	EARLY DAYS		TRANSITION					MISSIONARY EXPANSION			
		6:1	8:1	9:1	9:32	11:24	12:25	16:10-17	20:5—21:18	27:1	28:16
LUKE'S SOURCES	Peter & John, Mark, Mnason and others, plus written sources		Paul & Philip	Philip	Paul	Peter	Paul and/or Barnabas	"WE" "WE" "WE" Luke may have observed much of this entire action firsthand. P A U L			

3) The remainder of the source material for Acts concerned the early days of the church. Most of it was probably secured orally from other sources, such as Barnabas, Philip, Peter, James, John, Mark and Mnason (cf. Acts 21:16). Luke probably consulted with them at such cities as Jerusalem, Antioch of Syria, and Caesarea.

IV. RELATION TO THE THIRD GOSPEL AND THE EPISTLES

Originally, Luke's two writings—his gospel and the Acts—probably were circulated as one work, since the narrative of his Acts was the natural sequel to the story of his gospel. But when John's record was published as the final gospel at the end of the first century, Luke's gospel was weaned from Acts and linked with the other three to become known corporately as "The Gospel."[7]

[7]This was a natural fusion, since all four books recorded the same message, though from four different vantage points. W. Graham Scroggie compares the Gospels with the other twenty-three books of the New Testament thus:

Gospels	Acts—Revelation
The Christ	The Church
Introduction of the Gospel into the World	Progress of the Gospel in the World
Christ for Us	Christ in Us
Christ Revealed Historically	Christ Revealed Mystically

Chart adapted from *Know Your Bible* (London: Pickering & Inglis Ltd., n. d.), II, 59.

At about the same time, Paul's writings were being collected and identified under the one title, "The Apostle." Thus seventeen New Testament books were brought together and reduced to two units. Moreover, these two units found their common link in Acts.

RELATION OF ACTS TO THE NEW TESTAMENT

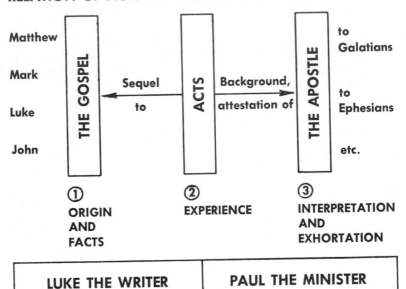

The genuine authenticity of Luke's gospel is shared by Luke's Acts because of the one author. And, since Paul's conversion and divine call were reported by Luke in Acts, the message of Paul's letters ("The Apostle") was thus given a strong acceptance. Furthermore, Acts also provided evidence of the apostleship of other New Testament writers, such as Peter and James. So in a very real sense Acts served as what F. F. Bruce has called the pivotal book of the New Testament. At the same time it must be recognized that this vindicative purpose of Acts was not one of the main reasons why it was written. These reasons will be discussed later.

The background which Acts provides in furnishing a setting for the Epistles—Pauline and General—is not small. It records such background as (1) the first Christian contacts with people to whom letters of encouragement and instruction were written later (e.g., I and II Corinthians, Ephesians); (2) the experiences of Paul during which some of his New Testament letters were written (e.g., I and II Thessalonians, written on his second journey from Corinth [See Acts 17]; and Philippians, written when Paul was imprisoned at Rome); (3) the introduction of men and women of Paul's acquaintance who appear in his letters (e.g., Timothy, Titus); and (4) general background of the reception given to the gospel around the Mediterranean world and the problems attending its proclamation (e.g., the persecution of saints in I and II Peter, and the troublesome legalists in Galatians).

V. PURPOSES

Three words may be used to suggest the overall *grand* purposes of Acts:

Registration
Vindication
Edification

Let us look at each of them with the view to enhancing our approach to the study of this inspired book of God.

A. *Registration*

The written record of the history of redemption comprises a substantial part of both the Old and New Testaments. The experiences of individual believers as well as those of the corporate people of God, are registered in the Bible, thus demonstrating before the audience of the ages that redemption is real, dynamic and worthy to be sought. God moved Luke to record the narrative of the early church in the Holy Scriptures in order to show the church's relation to (1) the past (continuation) and to (2) the future (propagation).

1. *Continuation.* Luke's own words reveal this aspect of the narrative. His purpose in the third gospel was to record, like the writers before him, the origins of Christianity: "to draw up a narrative concerning those matters which have been fully estab-

lished among us," (Luke 1:1, ASV, with marginal reading). The
first verse of Acts, by citing "all that Jesus *began* . . . to do and
teach" implies that Luke intends to show how Acts *continues*
the story of Jesus as the ascended, exalted One (Acts 1:2, 9).

2. *Propagation*. Throughout Acts the thrust is one of extension,
propagation, multiplication and advance. Externally, the advance
is from Jerusalem to Rome; internally, it moves from a Jewish
hearing to a universal audience. While there is the backward
look to the origins, there is always the forward look to the waiting
work. The gospel had recorded the sacrifice of Jesus' life. Acts
now records how the Holy Spirit imparts that life to man.
The ORGANISM of the church is shown to be spiritual. Having
been born with Holy Spirit baptism at Pentecost, it produces new
life in miraculous conversions, and advances in power and influence so that at the close of Acts the word of the gospel is
preached unhindered even from prison. (The last word of the
Greek text of Acts is *akōlutos*, "without hindrance.") The OR-
GANIZATION of the church is also given prominence by Luke.
It begins small, so small that the church in Jerusalem can meet in
private homes. The environment then is more or less homogene-
ous. But with advance and enlargement there is a corresponding
growth in organization, though fortunately never larger than the
need. Offices are created to promote efficiency and virility within
the church in its varied ministry (e.g., caring for widows as well
as teaching the Word). A central council at Jerusalem deals with
the major problem of the religious barrier between Jew and
Gentile, as the issue is carried over into the Christian community's
doctrine of salvation. A local church organizes and supports a
foreign missionary program as geographical boundaries are over-
stepped. The peaceful, self-vindicating program of the evangel
so establishes itself, leaving clean footsteps wherever it goes, that
even the political powers of the provinces and empire give it
the needed protection in the face of the religious fanatics who
would destroy it. All in all, the church makes fantastic progress
in its first three decades of life, and Luke accurately registers this
phase of its history.

B. *Vindication*

Acts was written soon after the last event of its narrative. Why was there no delay or waiting period, as with the Gospels? As we approach the question we must recognize that although each book of the Bible was written primarily for the ages, its publication date was ordained by God so that its message could fill a contemporary need as well. A study of the times in which Luke wrote reveals that apparently Acts was given to the Roman world to let the history and message of the church *vindicate its claim to divine origin.* It needed to make clear to the Roman government that Christianity was not to be associated with Judaism, though both claimed the same God and same Old Testament Scriptures. In fact, Luke emphasized in Acts that the leaders of Judaism considered Christians as heretical and blasphemous, and that this formed the basis for most of the persecutions of the disciples of that day. There was a divine purpose in such a clarification of identity of the church at this time, for in just a few more years rebellion of Jewish authorities against the Roman Empire would lead to war, eventually culminating in the destruction of Jerusalem (A.D. 70) by the Romans. Thus Rome would know that the Christians were not part of any rebellion brewing against the empire.[8]

C. *Edification*

The prime purpose of Acts must have been for edification, for it was inspired and written to profit for teaching, reproof, correction and instruction in righteousness—a ministry of edification of the church of God. A soul may learn how to be saved from Acts, but the book was written primarily for the believer's instruction in how to live and serve God. Your study of Acts should be geared to learning what the book teaches about Christian living and the mission of the church of which you are a part.

If you were to make a list of problems facing the church and Christians today, you no doubt would be surprised to find that

[8]See F. F. Bruce, *Commentary on the Book of the Acts* (Grand Rapids: Wm. B. Eerdmans Publishing Co., 1954), for a discussion of this apologetic purpose of Luke.

Acts offers solutions to most—if not all—of them. Consider for instance such critical current problems as:

1) dimmed vision of the desperate need of lost souls and of the untapped resources made available by a miracle-working God

2) dearth of that total consecration where life and possessions are considered expendable in the hands of God

3) diluting the message of redemption by not distinguishing between new birth and social uplift

4) deceptions of Satan in his ever-new devices of opposition to God's work

5) diversity of spiritual needs and situations, demanding a flexibility and adaptibility of missionary methods

6) dynamic of personal evangelism in jeopardy whenever an engagement of mass evangelism is not supplemented by a vital follow-up program

The Survey Study of this manual (Part II) will suggest the major spiritual emphases of Acts, and so these will not be stated here.

VI. UNITY OF ACTS

There can be no serious question that the book of Acts is a single historical unit of composition. From beginning to end there is a continuity of narrative as to time references, historical events, leadership in the church, geographical extension and convert multiplication. All point to the one theme of the birth and growth of the early church.

As to the ending of Acts, some hold that the present text lacks an adequate conclusion,[9] brought about by any one of various possible circumstances as: (1) original ending has been lost, (2) Luke died before completing the work, (3) the great fire of Rome (A.D. 64), (4) political discretion, (5) Luke intended to write a third history, picking up the narrative from the last chapter of Acts.[10]

But actually, there is no sound reason for not accepting the

---

[9]Wm. M. Ramsay says, "No one can accept the ending of Acts as the conclusion of a rationally conceived history." St. Paul the Traveler (Grand Rapids: Baker Book House, 1951), rep. ed., pp. 351-52.

[10]This last view is proposed by Ramsay, op. cit., p. 352.

present ending as Luke's intended, artistically composed conclusion to his masterpiece. Consider the following:

1) Luke's narrative proceeds from Jerusalem to Rome; the closing note is Paul's unhindered preaching of the gospel from Rome (Acts 28:30-31).

2) A record of the acts of the early apostles could have gone on indefinitely, but some cutoff point needed to be determined. Luke, by inspiration of the Holy Spirit, ended the account on the triumphant note of Paul's preaching.

3) Regardless of when Paul died and when Acts was written, the remainder of Paul's biography, including his last years and death, is omitted by intention. No individual man in the book is the hero; nor is the church dependent on men. (Notice also how Peter, the other key man of Acts, fades out of the account at 12:17 to reappear only once again, at the Jerusalem Council, Acts 15.) Clearly this book is really the record of acts of the Holy Spirit.

4) In one sense the book closes with the suggestion that the whole story of Christianity has not been recorded. Again, this is by intention. For one thing, Luke probably wrote soon after the last event, so there was no more to write. But this would, by intention, emphasize the truth that the work of the church continues. The church may have its epochs, such as birth, persecution and revival, but it shall continue on until its work is done at the Lord's coming.

* * *

Thus, God has used Luke to give the church an inspired book about its beginnings. It is a book that has left no question about the church's origin, message, methods, power and ultimate destiny. It is the missionary's manual par excellence. It is the Christian's guide to being Christ's witness. It is your book, so study it diligently!

Part Two

SURVEY STUDY

SURVEY STUDY

PICTURE THE WHOLE; then analyze the parts. This is the correct procedure for in-depth Bible study. To scrutinize isolated verses without having seen the complete context is to forfeit the richer experiences of Bible study. Survey should always precede analysis in order to obtain an overall perspective, a general idea of the major emphases of the biblical book, and an orientation to the surroundings of the component parts which will be subsequently analyzed.

Your attitude in the initial stages of survey should be one of expectancy and patience. Without expectancy, your vision will be dimmed and golden nuggets will be overlooked unknowingly. Without patience, you will become bogged down in discouragement over unfulfilled expectations or in the weariness of reading much material without a corresponding proportion of quantitative demonstrable knowledge.

The survey or "skyscraper view" study of Acts suggested in this and the following chapter follows the general order shown by the accompanying chart:

Your experience will be this	The order of your study should be this	Your aim is this
PROCESS OF ACCUMULATION	STEPS	PROCESS OF ORGANIZATION
You move from first impressions to repeated impressions to enduring impressions	1) First reading 2) Second reading 3) Further studies 4) Recording the survey	To proceed from the random and indefinite to the organized and defined

Now gather your basic study tools (text of Acts, pen and pencil, and paper) and proceed with your survey study.

I. STEP ONE: FIRST READING

This is the cursory, one-sitting reading of the whole book of Acts, intended to break the ice, launch you on your project and give a taste of good things to come. The average reader can read the book in about ninety minutes, or approximately three minutes per chapter.

A. *Reading*

1. *Fresh Approach.* You probably have read Acts many times. Read it this time as though you had never read it before, in order to awaken your heart and mind from the dangerous sleep of letting the fantastic earth-shaking story of the evangel become commonplace, trite and ordinary.

SUGGESTIONS

As you read, alert your mind to the eternal implications of the things Luke wrote.

Visualize the setting of the early church; remind yourself of those things presented earlier in this book (chapter 4).

Remember that what you are reading was once written by the man Luke. Bring together the event of his pen and your eye.

If possible, read aloud, especially if you have never done this. The newness of such a procedure can help you immeasurably.

For this reading only, you may choose to use a modern free version of Acts which you have never used to understand the flow of the narrative.

Don't slow down in your first reading; this will be a constant temptation.

2. *First Impressions.* First impressions are not always enduring, nevertheless, they are necessary. You should always seek to be impressed, although you don't need to ask yourself in machinelike regularity, "How does this impress me?" The question is pertinent at the close of your reading; during the course of reading, maintain a spirit of openness and pliability so that you can be impressed.

B. *Recording*

Jot it down! It is important to immediately establish the habit of writing things down. Whether you use a notebook or separate sheets of paper, whatever you record throughout your entire study of Acts should be kept together for present and future reference. This is one tangible and fruitful way to draw dividends from your investment of precious time.

SUGGESTIONS

Holding a sheet of paper horizontally, draw a horizontal line in the center from margin to margin, labeling it thus:

| 1 | 5 | 10 | 15 | 20 | 25 | 28 |

Dividing Acts into these five-chapter sections is arbitrary and even artificial. But it provides identified locations in which to jot down, above or below the line, whatever you wish to record tentatively. (The real divisions of Acts will be determined later.)

Things to record:

1) your first impressions. Some may have no direct relation to a specific location in Acts; simply record these impressions at the top of the paper.

2) atmosphere. This may be the atmosphere of the book as a whole, or of its separate parts. Atmosphere words such as "hate," and "activity," are tone or setting words. Aim at one-word identifications.

3) key words and phrases. You may not find many of these in your first reading. But you will notice some. Record these at the bottom of your page.

4) key persons and events. Don't record everything here—only the major items.

5) personal notes and marks. The Bible you use for your study should be one in which you will not hesitate to make notations and markings. The paper texture and column space of the New American Standard Bible is very suitable for this. Throughout your study continue to make whatever notations are meaningful

and helpful to you. During this first quick reading you will have
opportunity to make only a few of these notations.

6) other observations. Throughout this manual suggestions of
areas of study are given to help you on your way. The manual's
ultimate purpose is to train you not only to observe but to know
for yourself in what directions to look. Therefore, begin now to
develop and use your own ingenuity and originality regarding
what to look for in Bible study. This is what is meant by the
phrase, "other observations," when it is used throughout the
manual. These observations are uniquely yours, and an active
participation in this realm will enhance your study immeasurably.

II. STEP TWO: SECOND READING

From the first reading you have gained a view of the highlights
of Acts, as Luke the author has given them preeminence by various literary devices such as repetition, progression and vocabulary.[1]

In your observations you may have detected the following atmospheres: opposition followed by defense, the hustle of continuous activity, triumph in adversity, a momentum of progressive
accomplishment, the disciples' ever-present compulsion to preach.

Your observations may have included: the many shifts of geographical setting, the Jews always stirring up opposition, the
many sermons recorded, the boldness of the disciples, the prominent place of the Holy Spirit in the apostles' lives, the many defenses of Paul in the last chapters.

Your list of key words and phrases may have included: "and it
came about," "but when," "preached," "boldly," "Jews," "Greeks."

All that you have gathered in the first reading—consciously or
otherwise—is preparation and groundwork for the second stage of
survey, the second reading.

The second reading of Acts should proceed more slowly than
the first, and yet not too slowly. With this reading things will
begin to crystallize and fit into a pattern, though that pattern
may still not be too clear. The kind of observations you make

[1] The individual words of the Bible are the basic ingredients of the divine
revelation. Considering the importance of the truths revealed, one can appreciate the factor of the Holy Spirit's activity in inspiring the human authors to choose accurate and appropriate words, as well as interesting ones.

here will be like those of the first reading, though they will be more thorough and definitive. Also, since your reading will be slower, you will want to make more notations in your Bible, such as underlining or circling strong phrases in the text which strike you are being very significant (e.g., "the Council saw his face like the face of an angel," 6:15b).

The major project of your second reading should be the securing of chapter titles, which should serve not as an outline of the book but as clues to the content of each chapter. When chosen with this in mind, the sum of them represents a condensed picture of the general flow of the book's message. Characteristics of a good title are:

1) preferably one word, not more than three.

2) picturesque words if possible (there are exceptions: e.g., a personal name like Stephen for chapter 7; and geographical names).

3) words taken directly from the text; not a paraphrase.

4) no duplication or similarity of titles.

5) words which tell you where you are in the book.[2]

A. *Identification of Segments*[3]

Occasionally chapter divisions in the Bible do not coincide well with thought divisions. Therefore, the analysis could be placed at a slight disadvantage if one used these chapter boundaries in a unit study during the analysis stage.[4] Before beginning the analysis stage you must check the chapter divisions. You may choose to do this during the survey process while you are securing your segment titles. (Actually, this manual's analysis lessons will identify segments for you, nevertheless you should personally pursue this part of your survey study.)

[2]Obviously, a phrase chosen as a chapter title may not depict the content of the entire chapter, but it should explicitly relate to a leading thought.

[3]The term "segment" is used in this manual to identify a unit of study, whether that unit is the length of one chapter, longer, or shorter. The term is used more often in the analytical stages of study than it needs to be used here in survey study.

[4]Notice, for example, how the American Standard Version connects Exodus 6:1 with 5:22-23, dissolving thereby the printed chapter division. Actually, most chapter divisions in the Bible are well placed. Many of the adjustments made for analysis are arbitrary, and may vary from student to student. Some of the variations suggested here are of an arbitrary nature.

As you read each chapter of Acts, satisfy yourself that the chapter division may be retained. Make no changes without good reason. The study plan of this manual is based on the following five changes (each reference indicates the *beginning* of a segment):

1) 8:1*b*—The phrase of 8:1*a*, "And Saul was consenting unto his death," is appropriately associated with the end of the Stephen story.

2) 9:32—Chapter 9 gives the story of Paul's conversion. Verse 31 is a fitting conclusion to that story; verse 32 picks up the Peter account again, therefore it seems logical to begin a new segment here.

3) 15:36—Paul's second missionary journey begins at this point; thus, it is well to make a division here.

4) 18:23—The start of the third missionary journey is almost obscured in the narrative. A new division (and therefore new segment) is necessary here.

5) 21:18—The point one chooses to distinguish between the end of the third journey and the subsequent events at Jerusalem is rather arbitrary. We shall use 21:18 as the beginning of the new section.

B. *Recording Your Segment Titles*

Since your survey chart will contain your segment titles, you should prepare the framework of that chart now. It should be similar to the accompanying chart (examples of segment titles are shown; you are to use your own titles). A sheet of paper 8½″ × 11″ held horizontally is adequate. Use most of the sheet for your chart, locating the base line at about the middle of the page.

Now go through Acts and secure your segment (chapter) titles. As you read, make observations and notations as suggested earlier. At the end of each chapter decide what segment title you will use to identify the chapter; then record the title on your survey chart. When you have chosen titles for all the segments of Acts, scan the list and try to visualize the flow of the narrative from beginning

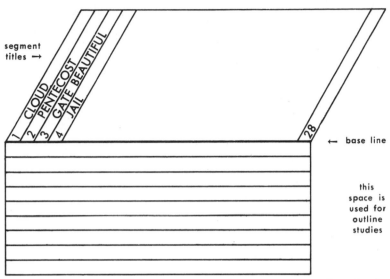

segment
titles →

CLOUD
PENTECOST
GATE BEAUTIFUL
JAIL

1 2 3 4

28

← base line

this
space is
used for
outline
studies

to end. You now will begin to sense a movement or flow in the narrative of Acts.

Your survey thus far has been of a groundwork quality. From this point on the outline of Acts is what you will seek.

III. STEPS THREE AND FOUR: FURTHER SURVEY STUDIES AND RECORDING THE SURVEY

Having seen the content of individual chapters, your task now is to determine Luke's organization of his narrative. It would be an oversimplification to say that since Acts is history Luke simply followed the chronology of events and recorded them in diary fashion. Remember that Acts does not exhaustively record everything that transpired in the first decades of the early church. Luke, inspired of the Holy Spirit, selected the events and items he would include to best serve the book's purposes. Selectivity and nondiarylike composition plus the inclusion of many sermons and addresses happily afford the potential of all the beauty, interest and appeal that can be found in a true literary work.

This part of your study does not involve another reading of the entire book of Acts as such. Instead, you will find that you must continually page through the book or certain sections of it as you proceed from subject to subject. Record the results of your studies on your survey chart as you proceed.

A. *Groupings of Chapters*

The easiest way to begin the search for Acts' organization is to identify groupings of chapters as determined by similarity of subject. In history, the three items of persons, events and places usually steer the narrative. Consider each of these separately, using the following questions as directive helps in locating groupings.

1) Who is the main character of the first few chapters of Acts? What was his title or work? How long does he stay in the narrative of Acts?

2) Who is the main character of the last chapters? Where is he first introduced? At what chapter does he reappear to remain the key person?

3) From your study thus far, is any part of Acts not represented by a main character? Record all your findings thus far on a line drawn under the base line of your survey chart:

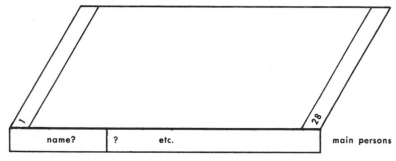

4) Now try events. We have already spoken of Paul's missionary journeys. How many were there? Where did each begin and end? Locate them on your chart. If Paul was not always on missionary journeys in Acts, account for the remainder of his Acts years and organize the study on your chart. Repeat this study for Peter's life, earlier in Acts.

5) Consider the events of the church. Does Acts record its beginning? Where? Then what were its periods of experience? (Note: You do not record on your survey chart individual items

of the subject you are studying. You are always after groupings. Hence the question just given does not ask for experiences, but periods of experience.)

6) Evangelism is a prominent theme in Acts. In the early chapters of Acts the gospel was generally preached where and to whom? On Paul's missionary journeys? Was there a change in audience, generally speaking? What do chapters 10 and 11 contribute to your answers to this question?

7) You have already observed that geography plays a vital part in Acts, especially in terms of the expansion of the gospel. Consider where Acts begins and where it ends. Relate this to 1:8. Using the geography of this verse as an outline, identify the three geographical sections on your survey chart with the appropriate dividing points.

8) Other survey studies either may be made now or reserved to a later time in your project. Two suggested subjects are: "Persecution," and "Progress of the Gospel."

B. *Major Movements*

Progress in some direction is the normal pattern of composition. The book of Acts is no exception. From what you have already read and studied of Acts, try to identify its major movements. You have already noted the geographical expansion of the gospel witness. In the account does persecution increase, wane or remain constant? Is there a climax of any sort in the book? Look also for turning points or strategic centers about which the narrative pivots. Are there any transition sections or any notable contrasting sections?

Use your ingenuity in recording the results of this study of movement in Acts on your survey chart.

C. *Theme and Key Verse*

In his gospel Luke explicitly revealed the theme of the narrative by telling his purpose in writing (Luke 1:1-4). John did the same for his gospel (John 20:31) and for the Apocalypse (Rev. 1:1). Usually, however, such a theme is not explicitly given. It might be said for Acts that while there is one major theme (the

ACTS

Author: Luke
Date Written: A.D. 61
Key Word: Witness
Key Verse: 1:8

THE FIRST THREE DECADES OF THE WITNESS OF THE GOSPEL

Acts of Peter | Acts of Paul

Chapters / themes:

1 TAKEN UP
2 HOLY SPIRIT
3 GATE BEAUTIFUL
4 IN WARD
5 ANANIAS & SAPPHIRA
6 WIDOWS
7 STEPHEN
8:1b PHILIP
9:1 SAUL
9:32 —
10:1 CORNELIUS
11 DORCAS
12 PETER EXPOUNDED
13 HEROD / CYPRUS
14 LYSTRA
15:1 CIRCUMCISED
15:36 PHILIPPI
17:1 ATHENS
18:1 CORINTH
18:23 EPHESUS
20:1 FAREWELL
21:1 GIRDLE
21:18 ARREST
22:1 STAIRWAY
23 CONSPIRACY
24 FELIX
25 FESTUS
26 AGRIPPA
27 SHIPWRECK
28 ROME

A.D. 30	Church Is Born	Church Grows Through Testing	Church Is Scattered	Church Embraces Gentiles	Church Extends Overseas	Church's Leader on Trial
	30	33	37	47	49 52 56	61

Paul in Acts:
- Paul the Persecutor
- Paul Saved
- Paul Instructed

- Paul the Missionary
- Paul the Prisoner

Judea — Damascus — Arabia
Jerusalem | Judea & Samaria | Transition

Philip — Barnabas — Peter — Paul

First Journey | Second Journey | Third Journey | Jerusalem | Caesarea | To Rome

Uttermost Parts

Jewish Period — Gentile Period

P A U L

Church Established | Church Scattered | Church Extended

Peter

Jerusalem
Old Testament Jewish Period — Gentile World — Universal Gospel
Heritage

Rome

wording of which has numerous possibilities), there are other themes which may be just as important woven into the narrative. For example, the major theme of Acts may be worded in title form as "The Progressive Witness of the Gospel." One of the many other themes may be stated as: "The Acts of the Holy Spirit."

Write out a list of the many possible themes—major or otherwise—for Acts. Decide which one you want to use as the hub or center of your study. Reduce the wording of the theme to title form, and then record the title on your survey chart. Having the image of your chosen title always before your mind during analysis will help you to keep details clearly in focus as they are viewed in the field of the wide-angle view.

Having decided on a title, it should not be difficult to choose a key verse. Such a verse should support the title and therefore be representative of the overall scope of Acts. Record this verse also on your survey chart. For example, for the title "The Progressive Witness of the Gospel," a good key verse would be 1:8b: "And you shall be My witnesses both in Jerusalem, and in all Judea and Samaria, and even to the remotest part of the earth." (It often happens in survey study that the student decides on a key verse first, and then derives a title from it. Either procedure is proper.)

D. *Completing the Survey Chart*

The major studies of your survey of Acts have now been recorded. At this time other items also could be recorded, such as the key words and phrases which have turned up in your study thus far, and approximate dates of the events of Acts (you may wish to use those shown on the chart of page 52, or dates obtained from other extrabiblical sources[5]). As you proceed in your analytical studies of Acts, you may want to add other items to your survey chart. So although your survey chart as of now should be

[5]Dates throughout this study manual are for the most part approximate. For a good system of New Testament chronology, see the chart *New Testament Chronological Chart*, rev. ed. (1968), by James L. Boyer, studygraph edition by Moody Press, Chicago. Professor Boyer also gives a clear presentation of the factors which determine the assigning of dates to New Testament events.

substantially complete in order to provide orientation in the
course of analysis, it also should be open to additions later on.

The author's survey chart on page 52 is given as an example and
also to illustrate the author's plan, procedure and remarks of the
analytical lessons of the manual.

Part Three

ANALYTICAL STUDY

I. THE CHURCH IS BORN
   (1:1—2:47)

The Church's Work	(1:1-14)
The Church's Workers	(1:15-26)
The Church's Spirit Baptism	(2:1-21)
The Church's Gospel	(2:22-47)

II. THE CHURCH GROWS THROUGH TESTING
   (3:1—8:1a)

The Test of Popularity	(3:1-26)
The Test of Loyalty	(4:1-22)
The Test of Things	(4:23—5:11)
The Test of Fortitude	(5:12-42)
The Test of Responsibility	(6:1-15)
The Test of Grace	(7:1—8:1a)

III. THE CHURCH IS SCATTERED
   (8:1b—9:31)

Samaritans Saved	(8:1b-25)
An Ethiopian Saved	(8:26-40)
Saul Saved	(9:1-19a)
Saul's First Ministries	(9:19b-31)

IV. THE CHURCH EMBRACES GENTILES
(9:32–12:25)

Peter's Outlook Changed Through a Vision   (9:32–11:18)
Mission-minded Church at Antioch   (11:19-30)
God's Deliverance of Peter from Prison   (12:1-25)

V. THE CHURCH EXTENDS OVERSEAS
(13:1–21:17)

First Missionary Journey   (13:1–14:28)
Jerusalem Council   (15:1-35)
Second Missionary Journey   (15:36–18:22)
Third Missionary Journey   (18:23–21:17)

VI. THE CHURCH'S LEADER ON TRIAL
(21:18–28:31)

Paul Before the Mob and Council   (21:18–23:30)
Paul Before the Governors   (23:31–25:12)
Paul Before a King   (25:13–26:32)
Paul Reaches Rome   (27:1–28:31)

LESSON 1

THE CHURCH'S WORK

1:1-14

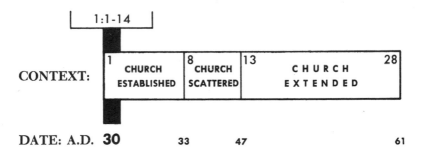

	1:1-14			
CONTEXT:	1 CHURCH ESTABLISHED	8 CHURCH SCATTERED	13 CHURCH EXTENDED	28

DATE: A.D. **30**   33   47   61

PLACE: Mount of Olives; Jerusalem

RULERS: Tiberius, emperor of Rome (A.D. 14-37)
　　　　Pontius Pilate, governor of Judea (A.D. 26-36)
　　　　Joseph Caiaphas, high priest (A.D. 18-36)
　　　　Herod Antipas, tetrarch of Galilee (4 B.C.–A.D. 39)

INTRODUCTION

ACTS IS LUKE'S COMPANION VOLUME to his book of the gospel and was written to tell the sequel to the gospel's story. "The first account" (Luke's gospel) was "about all that Jesus began to do and teach" (Acts 1:1), recording the works and words of Jesus' public ministry. The Acts account was not intended to duplicate this record but to supplement it by telling the continuing story of Christ's works and words in and through His witnesses. This is why the phrase of Acts 1:8 "you shall be My witnesses" is such an adequate key phrase of the entire book. Because this phrase appears in the book's first segment, the student gets a purpose-perspective at the outset of his study of Acts.

PREPARATION FOR STUDY

To prepare your mind and heart for the study of this first segment of Acts, mentally transport yourself to the post-resurrection days of Jesus when He ministered for forty days to His apostles and His other disciples in anticipation of leaving them. Follow the suggestions below to help you in this preparatory discipline.

1) Read the ending of Luke's gospel in chapter 24. Concentrate on verses 36-53. What was the disciples' problem when Jesus stood in their midst? (37-38). What two things did Jesus do to help them? (39-43; 44-49).

2) Picture yourself as one of the apostles: Jesus has died; and He apparently has risen again. What questions would now come to your mind? Keep in mind that earlier you as an apostle had forsaken your vocation to follow Jesus. Keep in mind also that as of this moment the kingdom of your expectation has not yet appeared.

3) If God intended the gospel of salvation for the world (e.g., read Luke's reporting of Simeon's words, Luke 2:28-32), then what was His design for the gospel's propagation as of the ending of Luke's gospel? Note verses 48 and 49. What is revealed here? What is not disclosed?

4) From this last chapter of Luke's gospel, describe the state of mind and heart of the disciples during the last days of Jesus' earthly career.

No matter how one may compare the apostles and other believers before Pentecost with the same group after Pentecost, one thing is certain: a transformation had taken place. The day of that transformation was Pentecost when Jesus sent the Holy Spirit. Before sending Him, however, Jesus chose first to identify the worldwide task which would confront His church (1:1-14), followed by His choosing the man to complete the team of apostles upon whose shoulders the leadership of the gospel's work would fall (1:15-26). The stage was being set in a real sense for the event of Pentecost, and Luke has recorded this in chapter 1.

5) Acquaint yourself with the context of this first segment of Acts. Acts 1:1-14 is the opening segment of the section Acts 1:1—

2:47, which we may call, "The Church Is Born." The five segments and an outline built around them may be identified thus:

THE CHURCH IS BORN
Acts 1:1—2:47

1:1	1:15	1:26	2:1	2:22	2:37	2:47
THE CHURCH'S WORK	THE CHURCH'S WORKERS		THE BAPTISM	THE SENDER	THE RESULTS	
			THE CHURCH'S POWER			
JESUS COMMISSIONS			HOLY SPIRIT ENABLES			
Jesus identifies the task	Jesus chooses a worker		Jesus sends the Holy Spirit			

ANALYSIS

A. *General Instructions*

Various methods of analysis are suggested in this manual. The
question-answer method is one of the prominent ones. In order
to encourage a methodical reconstruction of the author's composition of the biblical text to help in answering the various types of
questions, the analytical chart method of recording observations
is used in many of the lessons. Most of the methods outlined in
the steps below should be standard procedure for recording your
studies on an analytical chart. Learn the steps thoroughly in order to develop a methodicalness in your study habits. There are
basically six different kinds of study which you will want to record on your analytical chart. Refer to the chart on page 62 of
Acts 1:1-14; with its key to nomenclature given at the bottom
of the chart, as you read the following descriptions of those six
kinds. (Note: Only the biblical text appears within the rectangle;
your own words are recorded in the margins):

1) KEY CENTER. This is the key word or phrase of the biblical text which you choose as the basis of your main topical study. Notice on the chart how the key center is shown, by arrows, to relate to a phrase in each paragraph of the segment. The main topical study is comprised of key center, master title and paragraph points. Your main topical study may be used later as an expository outline of a subject in the segment.

2) MASTER TITLE. This title, in your own words, is derived from your key center, and expresses the main subject you are studying in the segment. (The main subject you choose need not necessarily be the main point of the biblical writer.)

3) PARAGRAPH POINTS. These points, one per paragraph, are actually subpoints under the master title. They represent, in your own words, the thought of the phrase of each paragraph to which you have already related the key center.

4) PARAGRAPH TITLES. These are words chosen from the text, picturesque if possible, to identify a paragraph at a glance.

5) SUPPLEMENTARY STUDIES. These are all other studies recorded in the margins. Some may be isolated observations; but you should concentrate on related paragraph-to-paragraph studies.

6) TEXTUAL RE-CREATION. The biblical text of the segment you are studying is recast on the chart, inside the $4'' \times 9''$ rectangle, and organized so as to show the real emphases and relations in the text.[1] The entire text need not be recorded. But you should include all words, phrases and verses that appear prominent in your early readings.

[1]Textual re-creation is the process of printing the biblical text on your analytical chart so as to reveal its thought and grammatical organization in a nontechnical manner. Such organization or structure involves relations of words to words and clauses to clauses, whether near or distant; cores of complicated sentences; distinctions between primary and subordinate phrases; listings of items; laws of composition; and many other structural items. The purpose of textual re-creation is to pictorialize the biblical text, letting it speak for itself by emphasizing the primary and de-emphasizing the subordinate. Various graphic aids used for textual re-creation include: indentations, underlining, large and small capitalizations, small-type letters, circling, boxing, various colors, arrows, numerical listings, blank spaces and color shading. (See *Independent Bible Study*, pp. 126-33 for author's description of textual re-creation.) Note: The extent of detail of your textual re-creation is optional. You may choose to do an abridged form of textual re-creation.

1. Organize your study tools: paper (one sheet for observations; one sheet for analytical chart), pens and colored pencils, and your Bible (New American Standard Bible recommended).

2. Draw a vertical rectangle (4"×9") on your analytical paper, dividing it into the three paragraph sections, as shown on the accompanying chart. Note that the size of the paragraph space is approximately proportional to the number of verses in the paragraph. Mark off the paragraphs in your Bible, if the version you are using does not so designate them.

3. Read Acts 1:1-14 in your Bible. As you read, underline key words or phrases that stand out for whatever reason. Try to read the story as though you have never read it before. (Test yourself by the following: a responsive reader, sensitive to the awesome implications of the gospel, would not be unmoved by reading the story of a miracle. Are there any miracles in this account?)

4. After your first reading, record a paragraph title (similar to segment titles described earlier in this manual) in upper right-hand corner of the paragraph section (such as is illustrated in the accompanying chart).

5. Read the text again. Begin more and more to think in terms of the three paragraphs. What is the one main thing Luke is trying to relate in each?

6. At this point in your study, if possible, choose a key center, the thought of which relates to a prominent thought in each of the three paragraphs. Underline the words or phrases in your Bible.

7. Now record your textual re-creation, including key center and other items on your analytical chart. Secure a master title for your study, derived from your key center. Proceed to record observations (especially observations of related or sequential items) on your chart as you continue studying the text. The suggestions and questions that are given below are intended to suggest areas or topics of study that should help you in your analysis. Don't go to helps for the answers; your Bible text will supply the answers to these questions. (Note: In order to furnish an illustration of an analytical chart, such a chart of Acts 1:1-14 is given with this lesson only. This, however, should not deter you from making your own original study of this segment, provided you keep

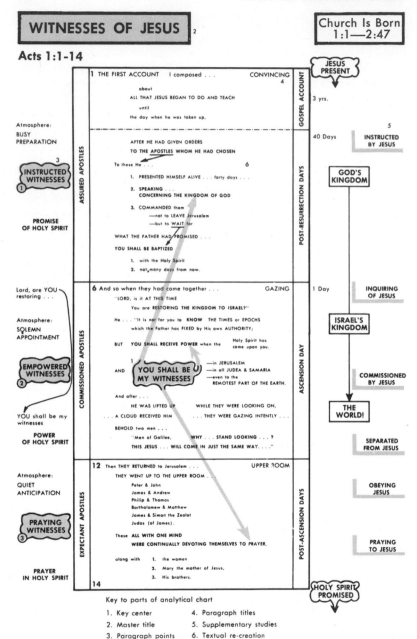

WITNESSES OF JESUS 2

Acts 1:1-14

Church Is Born
1:1—2:47

Key to parts of analytical chart

1. Key center
2. Master title
3. Paragraph points
4. Paragraph titles
5. Supplementary studies
6. Textual re-creation

from examining the illustrated chart too intently before you make your own analysis. Let it serve mainly as a format illustration.)

B. *Things to Observe*

(Record as much as you can on your analytical chart, always in condensed form. Aim at recording word and short-phrase observations; avoid sentence observations.)

1. Time periods of the paragraphs. Text may not be explicit; but the evidence is there.

2. Jesus as a main character. Identify His part throughout the segment. Also, what about His body?

3. Atmosphere: identify the general atmosphere of each paragraph.

4. Make paragraph-to-paragraph studies of:

> APOSTLES
> HOLY SPIRIT
> WITNESSES
> KINGDOM
> GEOGRAPHY

5. Are there contrasts in this segment? Is there a climax or turning point?

C. *Further Observations and Interpretations*

(Record as much of this as you can on your analytical chart.)

1. Paragraph 1:1-5. In verses 1 and 2 study the context of these three names: "Jesus," "Holy Spirit," "Apostles." What does this tell you about the subject of the book of Acts? If you have not already done so, record on your analytical chart, opposite the paragraph, the different things Jesus did during the post-resurrection period of forty days. How important was each? What does this reveal to you as to what may be considered the important things of the church's work?

2. Paragraph 1:6-11. Notice the phrase "kingdom to Israel." How had Jesus referred to the kingdom (1:3)? Why would Jesus wait to answer the apostles' question?

Compare "know" (v. 7) with "power" (v. 8) in the context.

Compare "You" (v. 6) with "you" (v. 8) in the context.

Compare "My witnesses" (v. 8) with "Men of Galilee" (v. 11) in the context.

What are the implications of the geographical commission of verse 8?

What is implied by the phrase "gazing intently" (v. 10)?

3. Paragraph 1:12-14. The statement "Then they returned to Jerusalem" (v. 12) seems ordinary. What important thing is involved?

Luke records the list of the regathered apostles in verse 13. Compare the list with those mentioned in Luke 6:12-16, Matthew 10:2-4 and Mark 3:16-19. Consider the importance of this gathering, keeping in mind where they have been and what they have been doing since they last met together in the upper room just before Jesus' arrest. In what sense is this verse a harbinger of good things to come? List some important lessons on prayer derived from verse 14.

4. After you have finished your analysis of this passage, go back and rehearse the various spiritual applications your study has revealed. Write these on paper, using the personal pronouns "I" and "me" whenever possible.

EXPLANATIONS

1) "Theophilus" (1:1). The name literally means "dear to God." The name was in common use from the third century B.C. onward. The title "most excellent," used for him in Luke 1:3, may have been in respect of his official rank (cf. Acts 23:26, 24:3, 26:25) or may have been a gesture of courtesy.

2) "Sabbath day's journey away" (1:12). The Jews interpreted Exodus 16:29 as allowing them to move about their city but not beyond it on the Sabbath. But did the outer boundaries of the city include the suburbs? Finding an answer in Numbers 35:5, the Jews combined the two verses and arrived at 2,000 cubits (3,000 feet) as the legal distance for a Sabbath day's trip. See also Joshua 3:4 for a reference to this distance; some feel this verse forms the basis of the Jewish tradition.

3) "The upper room" (1:13). This was a chamber in the upper

story of a large house. Bruce says it was generally used as a dining room or sublet to poor people.[2] Often the room was used as a hall for meetings of large groups of people (cf. Acts 20:8). Luke's use of the definite article "the" indicates that this upper room was a well-known place. In all probability this was the room of Jesus' Last Supper (Mark 14:15; Luke 22:12), therefore it may have been the house of Mary the mother of Mark (cf. 12:12).

FURTHER ADVANCED STUDY

(NOTE: These suggested studies in each lesson are optional; the continuity of the lessons is not dependent on their completion.)

1) Proofs of Christ's resurrection (1:3). Study Paul's classic discussion of Christ's bodily resurrection in I Corinthians 15:5ff.

2) Compare the question of verse 6, as to what was uppermost in the apostles' mind, with the later question of 2:37 and Peter's answer (2:38-39), as to what then was considered uppermost. What brought on the change?

3) The apostles were not only witnesses of Jesus; they were eyewitnesses of certain events. Of what key event? (Read Acts 1:22; 2:32; 3:15; 5:32; 10:39,41; 13:31; 22:15; 26:16; I Cor. 9:1.) It was vital for the successful mission of the early church that the key miracle, the grand miracle of the resurrection, be preached by those who personally saw the resurrected Jesus. One by one the eyewitnesses would die. Then with the gospel established, it would be the task of the witnesses of the succeeding ages to broadcast the message. Think of all the things involved in this word "witness." Use Isaiah 43:10; 44:8; 49:6; John 18:37 as guides to your study. Note from John 18:37 that Jesus' work was to bear witness to the truth.

4) "This Jesus . . . will come in just the same way" (1:11). Read these references to Christ's second coming: Mark 13:26, 14:62; Matthew 24:30, 26:64; Luke 21:27. What is the main emphasis of these prophetic statements?

5) Before Pentecost Day arrived, the apostles were engaged in prayer. Compare this with a similar situation at the beginning of Jesus' public ministry.

[2]F. F. Bruce, *The Acts of the Apostles* (Chicago: Inter-Varsity Press, 1952), p. 73.

6) With the use of a concordance, make a topical study of the word "kingdom" as it appears in Acts. Note especially 8:12; 20:25; 28:23-31. (For an excellent word study of "kingdom," read Gerhard Kittel's *Bible Key Words* [New York: Harper & Row, Publishers, 1958] Part III, II, 22-59.)

For the premillennial view of the kingdom, the following books are recommended: *The Kingdom in History and Prophecy*, Lewis Sperry Chafer; *The Greatness of the Kingdom*, Alva J. McClain; *The Basis of the Premillennial Faith*, Charles C. Ryrie; *The Millennial Kingdom*, John F. Walvoord.

The amillennial viewpoint is given by Oswald T. Allis in *Prophecy and the Church*. The post-tribulation interpretation within a premillennial system is presented by George E. Ladd in *The Blessed Hope*.

7) Note Luke's reference to women in verse 14. Luke is known for his tender respect for women, as revealed by his frequent references to them. Read Luke 7:36ff.; 8:2; 10:38; 11:27; 23:27, 29, 55; Acts 5:14; 8:3, 12; 9:2, 36; 13:50; 16:1, 13-14; 17:4, 12, 34; 22:4.

WORDS TO PONDER

"Why do you stand looking . . .?" (1:11)

Lesson 2

THE CHURCH'S WORKERS

1:15-26

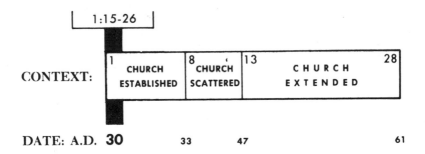

CONTEXT:

1 CHURCH ESTABLISHED	8 CHURCH SCATTERED	13 CHURCH EXTENDED 28

DATE: A.D. **30**   33   47   61

PLACE: Jerusalem

INTRODUCTION

THE ELEVEN MEN whom Luke cited in 1:13 were not common. These were men whom Jesus had chosen from the large group of disciples who were following Him, and whom He commissioned to be apostles ("sent ones"). (Luke 6:13: "And when it was day, he called his disciples: and he chose from them twelve, whom also he named Apostles.") Jesus trained them to be the first leaders of the church, the vanguard of God's army appointed to evangelize the nations. In the stress and bewilderment ensuing from Jesus' arrest and ignoble crucifixion they defected, denied and virtually disintegrated as a group. But, as we saw in the last lesson, the appearances of the resurrected Jesus brought them together again—"all were in place again, the panic past, and loyalty reborn."[1] All but one—Judas Iscariot.

[1]E. M. Blaiklock, *The Acts of the Apostles* (Grand Rapids: Wm. B. Eerdmans Publishing Co., 1959), p. 52.

67

PREPARATION FOR STUDY

1) Read the story of Judas' betrayal of Jesus in Luke 22:47-53;
Matthew 26:14-16. (Read also Ps. 41:9; John 13:18; 18:2-12.)
Then read the story of Judas' suicide in Matthew 27:3-10. For
Old Testament prophetical background to this, read Zechariah
11:12-13; Jeremiah 18:2; 19:2, 6, 11; 32:6-15; cf. Deuteronomy
23:18.

2) Read Acts 1:20. Then refer to the two psalms from which
the two quotations are taken (Ps. 69:25; Ps. 109:8).

3) Mentally reconstruct what activities you think the disciples
engaged in as a group while they waited in Jerusalem for the
coming of the Holy Spirit. Verse 14 has cited one thing. Had
they been instructed as of this time to proceed with any program
of evangelization? Concerning their organization, was anything
lacking at this time?

4) Keep in mind that the story of Luke at this point refers only
to the disciples and apostles in Jerusalem. Jesus had many other
disciples in other parts of the land, especially in Galilee. (For
example, it is held by some that Jesus' post-resurrection appearance of I Cor. 15:6 was made in Galilee.)

ANALYSIS

1) Remember to record things on your analytical chart as you
make observations along the way. (Note: Your analytical chart
rectangle is 4"×9" on the standard 8½"×11" paper; the skeleton charts shown in this and the following lessons are of necessity
out of proportion, due to the insertion of instructions on the bottom of the pages.)

2) Two paragraphs make up this segment (see chart). Read
the account with this in mind, getting your paragraph titles. What
is the major difference between the two paragraphs?

3) Read the segment again, underlining key phrases in your
Bible and watching for a key strategic phrase. After you have
found one which relates to other phrases in the segment, record
your textual re-creation, master title, paragraph points and so
forth.

4) Complete the suggested studies shown below the skeleton chart on page 70, recording all your findings.

5) Note the phrase "It is therefore necessary" (1:21). In what sense was the action necessary? Relate to a similar strong statement made earlier in the segment.

6) Paragraph 1:23-26. Note the three-step procedure used by the one hundred twenty brethren to determine Judas' successor. Was the method solely that of lots? Explain. Do many people today know about Matthias? What are your thoughts on fame?

7) List five spiritual applications which may be derived from this account.

EXPLANATIONS

1) "In their own language" (1:19). This was Aramaic, which had replaced Hebrew as the Jews' vernacular. The Hebrew as a vernacular had died with the Babylonian captivity, though it continued as the official religious language of the Jews and was spoken in the religious services.

2) "Barsabbas" (1:23). Joseph's surname is cited here to distinguish him from the many other Josephs. The little that is known today of Barsabbas and Matthias comes only from tradition.

3) "To his own place" (1:25). What do you think is intended by this phrase?

FURTHER ADVANCED STUDY

1) It is generally supposed that early in the experience of the Christian church a list was composed and circulated, containing the Old Testament passages which foretold events of the gospel narrative. The passage of this lesson indicates that the apostles were conversant with such prophecies. With the help of a concordance, make a study of the contexts of the phrase, "that it might be fulfilled" (and any similar phrase), as they appear in the New Testament. Arrive at conclusions from your own study.

2) Casting lots was an Old Testament procedure. Read the Old Testament verses cited in the margin of NASB that illustrate the method and the principles behind it. A concordance will offer other references. Note that the procedure of lots is not used again

Acts 1:15-26

ATMOSPHERE:

	JESUS' MINISTRY
15 JUDAS	
(Let your textual re-creation show Luke's parenthesis, and the Old Testament quotation.)	1 HIS DEATH
(Notice the ugly description of Judas' fate. Contrast this with the remainder of the segment.)	2 etc.
. . . Jesus went in and out among us	
(What five words of this segment are the strongest, in your estimation? Let your textual re-creation show this.)	
23 MATTHIAS	
And they . . .	
And they . . .	
And they . . .	
26	

◄ Use the narrow columns for topical outlines

1. Compare the very beginning and very ending of the segment, as to persons cited.
2. What is the overall atmosphere of the segment?
3. Make a sequential study of references to Jesus' ministry.
4. How much of the segment is about Judas? The remainder of the segment is about what? Outline this on your side narrow column.
5. Notice the strong words of 1:16. Make a related study of these.
6. Verse 16 refers to the words of David. In what verse are the words actually quoted? What does Luke record in between, and why? How much of verses 16-19 is Peter's speech? Luke's insert? Indicate this by your textual re-creation.
7. Notice all the words used to describe the office that Judas vacated. What were the qualifications for a replacement of that office?

in the New Testament record. (As you proceed in your study of
Acts, you will observe other things happening in the early chapters of Acts which do not appear again in the account. The issue
involved is, What is normative for the Christian church today?)
In what way might we say that the procedure of lot is based on
the principle of let? Defend the action of the disciples in drawing
lots at this time.

WORDS TO PONDER

"Thou, Lord, . . . knowest the hearts of all men . . ." (1:24).

LESSON 3

THE CHURCH'S SPIRIT BAPTISM

2:1-21

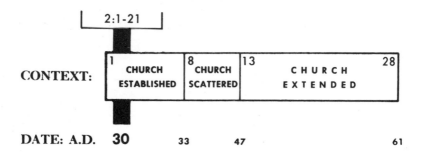

CONTEXT:

2:1-21		
1 CHURCH ESTABLISHED	8 CHURCH SCATTERED	13 CHURCH EXTENDED 28

DATE: A.D. 30   33   47   61

PLACE: Jerusalem

INTRODUCTION

THE APPARENT UNIFORMITY of nature and the slowness of change in the world make it exceedingly difficult for men to fully comprehend and feel the truth that many of the crucial events of God's timetable for mankind have been divinely designed to appear with abrupt suddenness, although they are announced beforehand. The seven days of repetitious marching around Jericho, following what must have been a monotonous pattern, ended in the split-second crash of the city's walls. The years upon years of Jeremiah's warning sermons to Judah came to an abrupt halt with the sudden assaults of the invading enemy hordes. The birth of Jesus, though foretold many centuries before, broke into the headlines, as it were, of a cold, dark, numb and degenerate generation with an abruptness very aptly represented by the angel's

72

sudden announcement to surprised shepherds going about their regular nightly chores (Luke 2:8-9).

After Jesus had ascended to His Father, His disciples had every reason to anticipate that both the coming of the Holy Spirit and the return of Jesus would be sudden events, not vaguely defined eras, whenever they would take place. This would be true of the Holy Spirit's coming, for (1) the event was clearly dated, "not many days from now" (1:5); and (2) Jesus' command for the apostles not to leave Jerusalem (1:4) until the Holy Spirit came would hardly have suggested an extended period of waiting. The Lord's return or second coming was also clearly identified by the two angels as a future moment of history, by the explicit announcement, "This Jesus . . . will come in just the same way as you have watched Him go into heaven" (1:11).

At this time the near event for the disciples was the coming of the Holy Spirit, and when He did come, it was suddenly (2:2). This is the story of the present lesson.

PREPARATION FOR STUDY

1) Acquaint yourself with the background of the phrase "And when the day of Pentecost had come" (2:1). First read Leviticus 23:15-21; then Exodus 23:16; 34:22; Numbers 28:26; Deuteronomy 16:10, 16-17. The word Pentecost comes from the Greek word for "fifty" (the "fifty days" of Lev. 23:16 reads *pentekonta hemeras* in the Greek Septuagint). The Feast of Pentecost was celebrated on the fiftieth day after the offering of the barley sheaf at the beginning of the Passover. The feast was also called Feast of Weeks (because of the period of seven weeks), the Feast of Harvest and the Day of Firstfruits.

Consider the purposes of God in choosing the Feast of Pentecost as the day when the Holy Spirit would be manifested in a new relationship to God's people. For one thing there would be multitudes of people in Jerusalem at the time, because of the "holiday" (this was a genuine "holy day").[1] But a more basic purpose was to show the spiritual association between the event of

---

[1]The Feast of Pentecost, celebrated probably during May, was one of the three great festivals of Jerusalem attended by Jews from all parts of the world.

the Holy Spirit's descent and the feast itself. Observe from your reading of the Old Testament passages (page 73) how the feast connoted rest from labor; thanksgiving for both material and spiritual blessing; holiness. Keep these in mind as you analyze Acts 2.

2) Locate on a map the places mentioned in 2:9-11. Observe that the visitors to Jerusalem had come from all points of the compass, and some from great distances. These are the Jews of the well-known dispersion, possibly numbering in the millions. From the days of the Old Testament captivities even to the present the Jews have been literally dispersed throughout the world.

3) Read from the Old Testament the context of Joel's prophecy which Peter quotes in Acts 2:16-21. In your reading of Joel, observe the progression of this outline:

Severe judgments	Joel 1:1–2:11
Call for repentance	2:12-14
Intercession	2:15-17
Lord's mercy and promise of restoration	2:18-27
Prophecies of the days "afterward"	2:28–3:21

ANALYSIS

1) First, notice the paragraph divisions of NASB. Keeping the paragraph structure in mind, read the passage through without interruption. Then return to a second reading, underlining key words and phases in your Bible.

2) Follow the general procedures for the analytical chart as outlined in Lesson 1, which include recording a main topical study, paragraph titles, textual re-creation, key center and supplementary studies. Continue your observing and recording by pursuing the lines of inquiry suggested in the remainder of this ANALYSIS section.

3) Each paragraph of this segment records a different aspect of the one story. Note how the three aspects are recorded on the skeleton chart shown (EVENT, REACTION, EXPLANATION). You will observe a pattern similar to this in other segments of Acts which follow. Are there any other ways in which the content of the paragraphs differ? Record these.

4) Now follow the suggestions shown below the skeleton chart

on page 76 recording on your own analytical chart the results of your studies. It is important to record observations in as few words as possible. Develop the knack of condensation, aiming at compact identifications wherever possible.

5) As you move into the interpretive stage, seek to answer any questions which your observations have raised. For example:

a) Why the phenomena of sight and sound in the first and last paragraphs?

b) Why would the Holy Spirit be identified with wind; fire; tongues? Try to recall other places in the Bible where the Spirit is associated with these items.

c) Compare the phrases "other tongues" (2:4) and "our own tongues" (2:11).

d) What is suggested by the picture language of the expression, "filled with the Holy Spirit"? (2:4). Relate the last phrase of verse 4 to this.

e) Could the prophecy of Joel have referred to more than just this one event of Pentecost? Justify your answer. Refer back to the Old Testament source.

f) What is the purpose of God in manifesting Himself or His work through signs and wonders?

g) What is the intent of describing the "day of the Lord" as "great and glorious" (2:20)?

6) In applying this passage of Acts, relate it to the unsaved, to the church[2] as a whole, and to the individual Christian. What is learned about God here? Make a list of your applications.

EXPLANATIONS

1) "Tongues as of fire" (2:3). This was not literal fire, but the appearance ("as of") was that of individual flames resting upon each of the disciples.

2) "Filled with the Holy Spirit" (2:4). In what sense were the disciples so filled? You will be studying the subject of the fullness

[2]This manual attempts to be consistent in representing the word "church" as referring to God's redeemed people as a whole (not limited to one generation) and also as representing more or less a geographically or temporally localized body of believers, e.g., the church at Jerusalem. The reader can determine by the usage of the word which concept is intended.

Acts 2:1-21

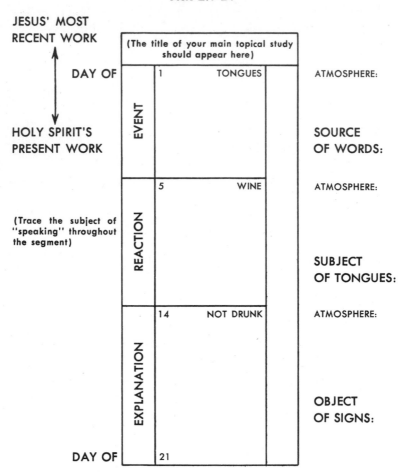

1. Make a study of the main actors of each paragraph.
2. Note how the segment begins and ends with references to "the day."
3. Identify the atmosphere of each paragraph.
4. Let your textual re-creation clearly show the *block* of Joel's prophecy. Note the different references to people in the prophecy. Emphasize in your textual re-creation the climactic statement of Joel.
5. Recall that witnessing is a key thought of Acts. Make a study of witnessing in this segment, as to its source, subject and object.
6. What does 1-4 tell about the apostles?
   What does 5-13 tell about the multitudes?
   What does 14-21 tell about God?
7. Relate this segment to the overall subject of Acts 1.

of the Spirit in more detail as you proceed in Acts. At this point it will be of great help to you to ponder over the implications, in view of the context, of this biblical phrase describing such a unique, initial experience of the early Christians.

3) "Began to speak with other tongues" (2:4). Would this be classed as a miracle?

4) "This sound" (2:6). To what does this phrase relate in the text?

5) "Asia" (2:9). This Asia was not the Asiatic continent nor Asia Minor, the latter term not coming into usage until the fourth century. The Asia of Acts is the west coast province of Asia Minor, as the NASB margin indicates.

6) "Proselytes" (2:10). See marginal note in NASB.

7) "In the last days" (2:17). When are the "last days"?

FURTHER ADVANCED STUDY

1) Study further the subject of speaking in tongues in Acts and I Corinthians 12:1—14:14. On the contemporary church scene the charismatic revival, identified outwardly by demonstrations of healing and tongues-speaking, is moving through many denominations. For help in evaluating this movement, refer to books on the Holy Spirit's ministry which treat the subject of the gifts of the Spirit (e.g., John F. Walvoord's *The Holy Spirit*, pp. 163-88).

2) Make a comparative study of the major speeches or sermons in Acts, listing length, subject, outline, method and appeal.

3) Study the use of the Old Testament in Acts, whether by Luke, or by the apostles themselves.

WORDS TO PONDER

"We hear them . . . speaking of the mighty deeds of God" (2:11).

LESSON 4

THE CHURCH'S GOSPEL

2:22-47

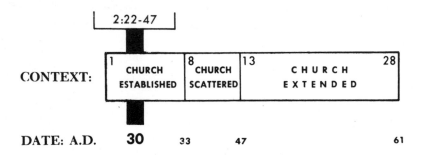

CONTEXT:

1 CHURCH ESTABLISHED	8 CHURCH SCATTERED	13 CHURCH EXTENDED 28

2:22-47

DATE: A.D. **30**   33   47   61

PLACE: Jerusalem: temple; houses

INTRODUCTION

THE PASSAGE OF ACTS studied in this lesson is in reality a continuation of that of Lesson 3, because Peter's sermon, beginning at 2:14, is not concluded until 2:36. The sequence of the Pentecost story is written by Luke in this order:

The Event—wind, fire, tongues 2:1-4
The Reaction—"What does this mean?" 2:5-13

Peter's Sermon[1]   The Explanation—"This is what was spoken of through . . . Joel" 2:14-21

The Arraignment—"This man . . . you nailed to a cross" 2:22-36

---

[1] The sermons or addresses of the early apostles generally followed a common pattern, and have since been called the *kerygma* ("proclamation," from the Greek *kerusso*, "to proclaim as a herald"). Bruce lists the parts of that

78

The last half of Peter's sermon (The Arraignment), which is a part of the text of this lesson, is the masterfully designed climax to a Spirit-inspired message. It is intensely personal and seeks to storm the wills of the listening Jews. What happened after the sermon was delivered is also the subject of our present study.

PREPARATION FOR STUDY

1) Peter's audience was predominantly Jews—"men of Israel" (2:22; cf. 2:36). Peter knew that although the events of this Pentecost Day were manifesting the person and work of the Holy Spirit, it was Jesus about whom he must speak. For the Jews did not reject the Spirit per se—but they had rejected Jesus as the Son of God and Anointed One, the Christ.

It was not difficult for Peter to get the subject of Jesus into his sermon about the Holy Spirit, for it was Jesus who had poured forth the Spirit, even as He had promised. But how could he convince the Jews that God had made Jesus both Lord and Christ? He would try by citing the witnesses, personal and impersonal. Your analysis will reveal the witnesses Peter used. You should be acquainted with the testimony of one of them, David, before you study the text. For this read Psalms 16:8-11 and 110:1.

2) To appreciate fully the blunt indictment which Peter laid to the Jews for their part in Jesus' death,[2] read afresh the gospel account of the ignoble and agonizing hours of the trial, scourging and crucifixion. But also keep in mind when reading Acts 2:22-36 that Peter is not charging the Jews alone with Jesus' death. The Jews are so cited because Peter is speaking to the Jews. Were he speaking to Gentiles, he would say that *their* sin nailed Jesus to the cross.

3) Peter's sermon is the first recorded sermon of the Christian era. As you study it, keep in mind that Peter had no idea what it would bring forth. Satisfy yourself as to what were Peter's motivations in delivering such cutting remarks.

pattern thus: (1) announcement that the Messianic age has arrived; (2) rehearsal of the ministry, death and triumph of Jesus; (3) citation of Old Testament Messianic prophecies; (4) call to repentance. F. F. Bruce, *Commentary on the Book of Acts* (Grand Rapids: Wm. B. Eerdmans Publishing Co., 1954), p. 69.

[2]Peter is careful to recognize that the Jews crucified Jesus in proxy, i.e., "by the hands of godless men," who were the Romans.

4) Mentally visualize the setting of Peter's preaching. The site is in the vicinity of the temple; the time, 9 A.M.; the audience, over three thousand Jews from all lands; the apostles are standing with Peter, the gesture itself being their consent to his words.

ANALYSIS

1) Follow the standard procedures of analysis already described in the preceding lessons. This includes recording your observations on the analytical chart. The present passage is longer than the previous ones, so you will find it advantageous in your textual re-creation to record only significant or strong phrases.

2) The section 2:22-36 is considered here as one paragraph, despite its length. This is because there is no real break in Peter's train of thought, though the Old Testament quotations may at first glance give that impression.

3) Note the three one-word identifications of the paragraphs as shown on the chart on page 82: Arraignment, Response, Results. Use your own outline if possible.

4) As suggested earlier, observe the witnesses which Peter uses (2:22-36) to attest that God had made Jesus both *Lord* and *Christ*. What do the words "Lord" and "Christ" signify?

5) Notice Peter's references to "men of Israel" (2:22) and "house of Israel" (2:36). There is no question therefore but that the Jews are Peter's audience. Keeping in mind the Jewish character, heritage and religious convictions as described in chapter 4 of this book, measure the strength of Peter's references to David and the frequent references to God and death.

6) From time to time in Acts, especially in the sermons and Old Testament quotations, you will find unusually long sentences. It often happens in such sentences that the main subject and verb are hidden in the grammatical complex of related clauses. You will find it a very enlightening experience in such passages to identify the "core" of the sentence, that is, the main subject, main verb and main object. Observe the long sentence of 2:22-23. You may pass by the first clause, "Men . . . words:" (which has a core by itself), since it is not the *primary* thought, content-wise. What is the core of the main section which begins with the word

"Jesus"? Compare this core with that of the short verse 2:32. What is the core of 2:33?

7) Now follow through on the study suggestions given below the chart on page 82.

8) Leaving the observation stage, continue your study in the areas of interpretation and application:

a) Concerning the references to the Holy Spirit, there is no explicit reference in the last paragraph. But what is the implied explanation of the situation described? What are the fruits of the Spirit?

b) Compare the fellowship of believers described in 2:42-47 with the pre-Pentecost group (1:12—2:1). Try to visualize this new fellowship of 3,000 believers staying "together" in their daily walk, as this passage describes it.

c) How do you account for such a tremendous response (3,000 souls saved) to Peter's sermon? What are the lessons here for Christian service?

d) In what way is the resurrection of Jesus related to the ministry of the Holy Spirit? How are both related to the Christian's living?

e) What were the essential points of Peter's explanation of the way of salvation (2:38-39)? Does Acts record all that Peter said (2:40*a*)?

f) From 2:41-47 compose a list of qualities of a true Christian fellowship.

EXPLANATIONS

1. "Jesus the Nazarene" (2:22). How was this an identification of scorn? Read Mark 1:24; 10:47; 14:67; 16:6; Luke 4:34; 24:19; Matthew 2:23; 26:71; John 1:46; 18:5, 7; 19:19; Acts 6:14; 22:8; 26:9.

2. "Hades" (2:27). "Hades" translates the Hebrew *sheol*, which was the Old Testament abode of the spirits of all the dead. There the righteous rested in bliss while the unrighteous endured endless torment.

3. "Gift of the Holy Spirit" (2:38). This is not one of the spiritual gifts which are imparted to believers (I Cor. 12:11); it is the Spirit Himself.

Acts 2:22-47

(Make a study of the Jews' relation-ship to:)				
SON	ARRAIGNMENT	22 DAVID		THE PREACHING OF ONE MAN
SIN	RESPONSE	37 3,000 "Brethren, what shall we do?"		PIVOT
NEW FELLOWSHIP	RESULTS	43 FAVOR 47		SALVATION OF THOUSANDS

1. Identify the main person(s) of each paragraph. This also will reveal the different subjects of each paragraph.
2. Notice how the atmosphere changes throughout the passage.
3. Observe the intensity of "Brethren, what shall we do?" In what sense is it a pivotal point in the narrative? Show how the narrative revolves about this. Describe what precedes and what follows.
4. Note names and titles used for Jesus throughout the passage; also note the references to His work. Record also on your chart what is taught about His resurrection.
5. Make a study of the Jews' relationship to the Son (first paragraph); to sin (second paragraph); and to the fellowship of believers (third paragraph).
6. Observe the references to the Holy Spirit and what is said of Him.

FURTHER ADVANCED STUDY

1. Study the context of the communal sharing of property and possessions (2:45), and account for the apparent disappearance of this activity as the narrative of Acts advances.

2. What light does 2:23 shed on the general doctrines of predestination and the sovereignty of God?

3. How do you explain the new converts' "favor with all the people" (2:47)? Account for the persecution that soon follows.

WORDS TO PONDER

"And everyone kept feeling a sense of awe" (2:43).

LESSON 5

THE TEST OF POPULARITY

3:1-26

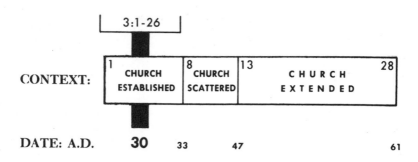

CONTEXT:

1 CHURCH ESTABLISHED	8 CHURCH SCATTERED	13 CHURCH EXTENDED 28

DATE: A.D.   **30**   33   47   61

PLACE: Jerusalem: Gate Beautiful; Portico of Solomon

INTRODUCTION

THE POPULARITY which the apostles and new converts enjoyed
was short-lived. Peter's Pentecost message about the resurrected
Christ had turned Jerusalem upside down in terms of the transformation of thousands of souls. In the homes, on the streets and
in the temple, this was the new topic of discussion, so that the
political and religious leaders, who sensed how such a spiritual
revolution would inevitably affect them, watched for the first
opportunity to nip this thing in the bud. The setting for their
appearance in Acts 4 is the lesson of Acts 3.

This new era of the people of God (the church[1]) began at
Pentecost. That was its birth. But babies must grow, and it was
in the design of God to let the church experience the pains and

---

[1]The word "church" does not appear in the original text of Acts until 5:11
(though the Western family of early manuscripts reads "in the church" for
2:47). A study of the word will be made at the appropriate time in Acts 5.

trials of its infancy in order to grow strong and build up a resistance to the Satanic viruses which would seek to destroy it. Chapters 3 through 7 describe a variety of such trials for the young fellowship of believers. Refer to your original survey of Acts, reviewing your chapter titles for Acts 3-7 and any outlines which you may have made for this section. Briefly scan through these five chapters of Acts with the following six segments in mind. These are the segments which will be studied in the lessons of this section.

THE CHURCH'S GROWTH THROUGH TESTING

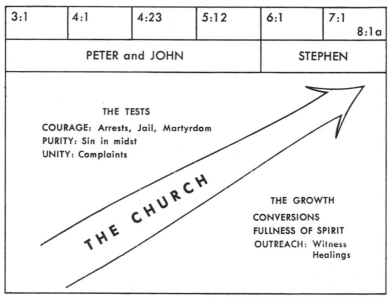

3:1	4:1	4:23	5:12	6:1	7:1 8:1a
PETER and JOHN				STEPHEN	

THE TESTS
COURAGE: Arrests, Jail, Martyrdom
PURITY: Sin in midst
UNITY: Complaints

THE CHURCH

THE GROWTH
CONVERSIONS
FULLNESS OF SPIRIT
OUTREACH: Witness
Healings

PREPARATION FOR STUDY

1. In order to visualize more keenly the action of this and other chapters of Acts transpiring in the area of the temple, study the accompanying structural diagram and ground plan of Herod's Temple, a magnificent structure begun in 19 B.C., usable by 9 B.C., and finally completed in A.D. 64. From the scale accompanying the diagram imagine the size of the mobs of people that could crowd into the many courts of the temple area. Read Mark 13:1-4 and Luke 21:5-7 for an insight into the grandeur and awe-

some spectacle of this great edifice. Refer to a Bible atlas for a map of Jerusalem which shows the temple's location in the city.

2. Read from the Old Testament the passages that Peter quoted in his sermon: Deuteronomy 18:15, 19; Genesis 12:3; 18:18; 22:18; (cf. also Lev. 23:29). Be sure to read the surrounding contexts of the verses.

3. Observe how the apostles usually were in pairs whenever they moved about in Acts. In this chapter Peter and John were together. Notice the listing of 1:13. Recall that Jesus sent out the seventy disciples two by two (Luke 10:1). What are the advantages of such a policy?

4. Keep in mind the commission for which the apostles are now responsible:

"You shall be My witnesses
. . . in Jerusalem . . . Judea and Samaria,
. . . remotest part of the earth" (1:8).

Observe that the apostles are not quickly leaving Jerusalem. The design of the commission did not call for this. Also, the apostles experienced many more things during the early post-Pentecost days than what Luke records in Acts. The events included are by selectivity, representative of the era of record.

ANALYSIS

1) The NASB divides this passage into only two paragraphs: the action (3:1-10) and the sermon (3:11-26). This reveals the simplest organization of the chapter. But you will find it helpful to divide Peter's sermon itself into at least two parts, with a new paragraph at 3:19; this is the basis for the analysis suggestions of this lesson.

2) Proceed with your usual readings, observations, notations and recording on the analytical chart. In your textual re-creation of paragraph 3:11-18, show how the phrase "His Servant Jesus" (v. 13) is the central phrase of the entire paragraph, to which the other verses point. This is the compositional law of centrality. Note in this connection also the core of verse 13.

3) Continue your analysis by following the suggestions given below the chart on page 89.

GROUND PLAN of HEROD'S TEMPLE

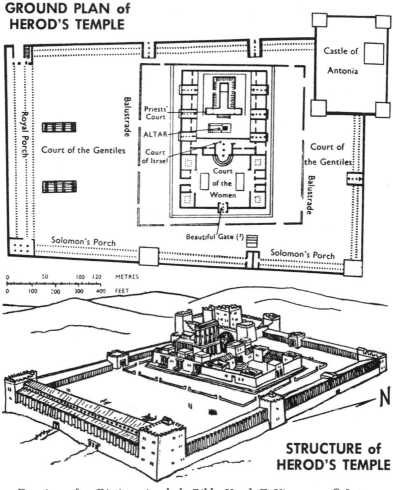

STRUCTURE of HEROD'S TEMPLE

Drawings after *Dictionnaire de la Bible*, V, ed. F. Vigouroux, © Letouzey et Ané, Paris. Reproduced by permission from the *New Bible Dictionary*, © Inter-Varsity Fellowship, London.

Note the following concerning the areas of the temple:

1. Jewish laymen were admitted as far as the Court of Israel.
2. Gentiles were allowed in the large outer court, Court of the Gentiles, which was not considered sacred ground as such.
3. Jewish women might enter as far as the Court of the Women. The treasury was also located here (cf. Mark 12:41-42).
4. The Priests' Court was reserved for the priests and Levites, and here they went about their services.

4) Interpretation and application

a) What lessons about Christian service are taught in the first paragraph? (There are more here than appear at first glance!)

b) Note Peter's reference to "our own power . . . piety" (3:12). How does he set these attributes in their true light by the attributes he ascribes to Jesus in 3:14-15?

c) Notice how Peter's message is interspersed with the nomenclature of the family household. (Note margins of NASB for "Servant," 3:13.)

d) Whose faith was the basis of the man's healing?

e) What do you learn from this lesson about:

Faith

Mercy

Repentance

EXPLANATIONS

1) "Hour of prayer" (3:1). Study Exodus 29:38-42; Psalm 55:17; Daniel 6:10 for background of this Jewish service.

2) "Gate . . . called Beautiful" (3:2). This bronze gate, also known as the Nicanor Gate, led into the Court of the Women, and probably derived its name from the exquisite beauty of its appearance.

3) "Entering the temple" (3:2). The reference here, as in other places, to people entering the temple is intended to mean entrance into the *courts* of the temple, surrounding the inner sanctuary.

4) "Prince of life" (3:15). The Greek word translated Prince is *archēgos*, meaning "pioneer" or "author" (NASB margin). This word appears in only three other New Testament verses: Acts 5:31; Hebrews 2:10; 12:2. Be sure to read these.

5) "Samuel" (3:24). Samuel was a prophet (I Sam. 3:20) whose words introducing David and his kingdom aptly described Jesus, the King of whom David was a type (cf. I Sam. 13:14; 15:28; 16:13; 28:17).

Acts 3:1-26

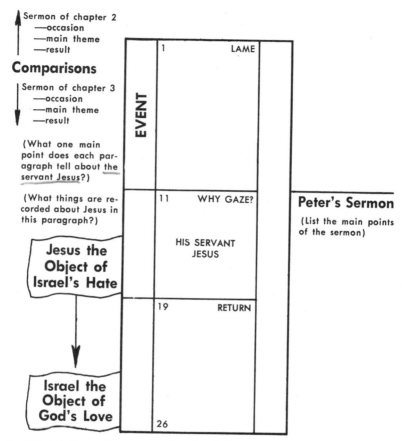

Sermon of chapter 2
—occasion
—main theme
—result

Comparisons

Sermon of chapter 3
—occasion
—main theme
—result

(What one main point does each paragraph tell about the servant Jesus?)

(What things are recorded about Jesus in this paragraph?)

Jesus the Object of Israel's Hate

Israel the Object of God's Love

EVENT

1	LAME
11	WHY GAZE?
	HIS SERVANT JESUS
19	RETURN
26	

Peter's Sermon

(List the main points of the sermon)

1. What is the main content of each of the two parts of Peter's Sermon? Record a one-word identification on the chart, completing the outline: EVENT; ....; ....
2. In what paragraph(s) is the idea of faith predominant? Repentance? Record in the narrow right-hand column.
3. Make a study of contrasts in this passage (e.g., what the lame man sought, and what he received).
4. Note how often the atmosphere changes in the first half of the passage.
5. In the last paragraph, note the different references to blessed things.
6. Let your textual re-creation of the last paragraph set off the Old Testament quote from the remainder of the text.
7. What is the strength of the first phrase of paragraph 3:19-26? Relate it to the last phrase of the paragraph.
8. Compare this sermon with that of chapter 2.

FURTHER ADVANCED STUDY

This would be an appropriate time in your study of Acts to consider the subject of "miracles" as signs attending the witness of the gospel. During Jesus' life on earth, what was His basic reason for performing miracles? Why were the apostles given the gift of healing? What likenesses are there between miracles today and miracles of New Testament times? Was the gift of healing in Acts a temporary or permanent spiritual gift? Recommended outside reading: *Miracles of Our Lord*, John Laidlaw; *Miracles*, C. S. Lewis; *Notes on the Miracles of Our Lord*, Richard C. Trench; *The Gospel Miracles*, Ronald S. Wallace.

WORDS TO PONDER

"I do not possess silver and gold, but what I do have I give to you" (3:6).

THE TEST OF LOYALTY

4:1-22

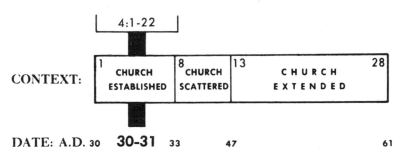

CONTEXT:

1 CHURCH ESTABLISHED	8 CHURCH SCATTERED	13 CHURCH EXTENDED 28

DATE: A.D. 30   **30-31**   33   47   61

PLACES: Jerusalem: jail and council (Sanhedrin) building near the temple

RULER: Caiaphas, presiding high priest[1] and leader of the council

INTRODUCTION

UP TO THIS POINT the apostles had not experienced any organized opposition. But after Peter finished his sermon with the cutting words "turning every one of you from your wicked ways" (3:26), and with John had continued speaking to the people (4:1), the religious authorities moved in. The reader can now begin to observe the workings of a system of government where the religious rulers have authority in the public domain, provided a religious issue is at least remotely involved. This was the arrangement between Rome and the Jewish nation, and the apostles were not exempt from the inevitable religious conflict. Interestingly enough, the occasions for Peter's two sermons were both

[1]Annas, father of Caiaphas, was formerly the high priest; now he is high priest emeritus.

91

very innocent and natural. Signs attending the Spirit's descent
called for an explanation; the people's near-idolizing of Peter
and John called for correction. The apostles were not looking
for trouble; they were merely destined to find it because of their
aggressive innocence in a God-given opportunity. And they were
prepared to confess their loyalty.

PREPARATION FOR STUDY

You will observe and understand more of this passage of Acts
if you first become acquainted with the official council or Sanhedrin[2] of Jewish rulers which were the apostles' opposition.

As the supreme theocratic court of the Jews, the council reflected the local autonomy which the Greek and Roman powers
granted the Jewish nation. Some important things to remember
about this council are:

1) Origin. The organization can be traced back as far as about
200 B.C.

2) Composition and organization. The council had seventy
members, plus the ruling high priest. Three professional groups
composed the council: high priests (the acting high priest and
former high priests) and members of the chief-priestly families;
elders (tribal and family heads of the people and the priesthood);
and scribes (legal professionals). At the time of Acts, two religious parties within Judaism were represented in this membership: the Sadducees of the majority and the Pharisees of the
minority. Caiaphas the high priest was a Sadducee. Most of the
scribes were Pharisees. The presiding officer of the council was
usually the high priest.

3) Administration. The council was connected with the minor
courts, being the highest court of appeal from these.

4) Extent of authority. Authority was broad and far-reaching,
involving legislation, administration and justice. There was religious, civil and criminal jurisdiction. In New Testament days

[2]The Greek word which NASB translates "council" is *sunédrion*, hence
Sanhedrin. This body was sometimes referred to as the Great Law-Court or
Court of the Seventy-One. (See 4:15 of NASB, and marginal reading.) At
times in the New Testament the Sanhedrin is referred to by such loose connotations as "rulers and elders and scribes," as Luke identifies the group at
4:5.

capital punishment required the confirmation of the Roman procurator.[3]

5) Sessions. In extraordinary cases the council met at the house of the high priest. Regular sessions were held daily, except on Sabbath and feast days, in a session room adjoining the temple.

* * *

As you approach this passage of Acts, try to keep in mind why the Jewish rulers and groups would object to what Peter has already preached. Only a few weeks had transpired since Annas and Caiaphas participated in Jesus' conviction (read John 18:12-32). Remember also that it was in the courts of the Jewish temple that Peter has talked about Christ and His resurrection.

ANALYSIS

1) This segment has three paragraphs, each one filled with intriguing facts to observe. Read through the passage aloud in one sitting, picturing the action as you read. Let the reactions of the opposition register in your mind. Note the desperate futility to which the enemy has been driven. Why would the Sadducees take the leadership of the opposition? (4:1). In the secret conference of the council (4:15-17), were arguments made against the *fact* of Jesus' resurrection?

2) Record your analysis on the 4″×9″ rectangle on page 95. The text of this passage is very productive in textual re-creation. Don't conceal any of the strong phrases.

3) Complete the outline already begun on the chart on page 95 (beginning with RESULTS), choosing words that will represent the main content of each of the other paragraphs.

4) Follow the suggestions at the bottom of the accompanying chart as you proceed to analyze the passage. You might refer now to that part of the EXPLANATIONS section identifying Caiaphas, Annas and others.

5) As you look for spiritual applications from this passage, consider the following:

   a) how Christian witnesses should act under the tension and fire of persecution (cf. also Luke 21:14ff)

[3]This regulation may not always have been followed diligently (e.g., the story of Stephen's stoning does not cite any action by the Roman authorities).

b) the secrets of spiritual power and confidence
c) the keynote of the gospel message
d) the simplicity of the way of salvation
e) the impotence of the enemies of God and the power of God
  to save

EXPLANATIONS

1) "Sadducees" (4:1). Study the following comparison:

COMPARISON OF PHARISEES AND SADDUCEES

PHARISEES	SADDUCEES
a) name meant "the separated ones"	a) name may be from *zaddikim*. "the righteous ones"
b) largest and most influential sect	b) second to Pharisees in prominence —majority power in council at this time —the aristocratic minority —educated and wealthy class
c) extreme legalism	c) external legalism
d) little interest in politics	d) major concern was politics
e) operated principally in the synagogues	e) operated principally in the temple
f) held these doctrines: immortality resurrection spirits and angels	f) denied: immortality resurrection spirits, angels
g) regarded rabbinic tradition highly	g) accepted as authoritative only the written Old Testament

2) "Rulers and elders and scribes" (4:5). This phrase refers
to the council (cf. "the Council" of 4:15). The elders and scribes
had special functions:

Elders. The elders of the Jewish community were official coun-
selors who, by right of first-born, succeeded to the headship of
a father's house, a tribal family or a tribe itself. Usually each
town had its elders. Because of their old age, their counsel and

Acts 4:1-22

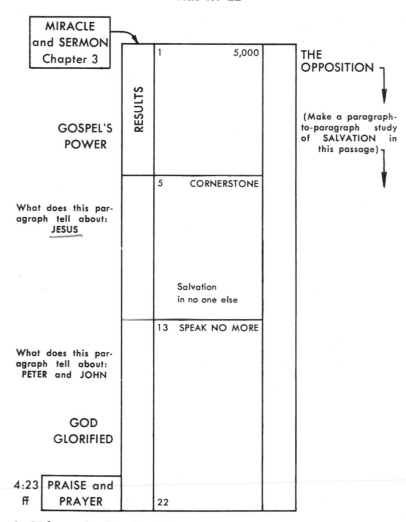

1. Make a related study of the opposition.
2. Observe the references to each person of the Trinity. What is the context of the references?
3. Note the context of the words "salvation" and "saved." When did Peter use the word "saved" before?
4. Contrast the beginning and end of the segment as to the rulers' power.
5. Notice the many contrasts in the short first paragraph.

decisions were respected. Their authority was undefined and extended to all matters of public interest. Their membership on the council gave it strong stature.

Scribes. The position of scribe was very highly respected in New Testament days. Scribes were the originators of the synagogue service. Their main functions were:

a) Study and interpretation of the law (civil and religious), determining its application to daily life.

b) Instruction of the law to a select group of pupils. The devotion of the pupils to their scribe was intense.

c) Administration of the law by their services on the council.

3) "And Annas . . ." (4:6). The first word of verse 6, "and" (*kai* in Greek), may be translated "including especially"; and then follows the names of the. key men of the council:

Annas: high priest from A.D. 6-15; deposed by the Roman governor; continued to enjoy great prestige; was the senior ex-high-priest of the council; may have presided over the council at times.

Caiaphas: son-in-law to Annas (John 18:13); was high priest from A.D. 18 to 36, when he was replaced by Jonathan, son of Annas.

John and Alexander: both were members of the chief-priest families; their exact identity is not known.

FURTHER ADVANCED STUDY

1) The Messianic prophecy of Psalm 118:22, quoted in 4:11, is one of the earliest of such prophecies. Make a biblical study of the word "stone" as it appears in the Bible, referring to Jesus either explicitly or by implication. Refer to such verses as Matthew 21:42ff; Luke 20:17ff; Mark 12:10ff; Isaiah 8:14ff; 28:16; Daniel 2:35; I Peter 2:6; Romans 9:33; Ephesians 2:20.

2) For outside reading on the ministry and services of the temple as they were at the time of Jesus, consult the following:

The Temple, Alfred Edersheim
The Temple and Its Teaching, Arthur E. Smith

Bible dictionaries and encyclopedias under the title "Temple": e.g., Hastings' *Dictionary of the Bible,* IV, 695-716.

WORDS TO PONDER

"Now as they observed . . . they were marveling, and began to recognize that *they had been with Jesus*" (4:13, with NASB margin).

Lesson 7

THE TEST OF THINGS

4:23–5:11

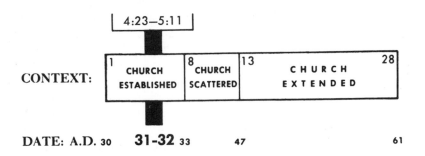

4:23—5:11

CONTEXT:

1 CHURCH ESTABLISHED	8 CHURCH SCATTERED	13 CHURCH EXTENDED 28

DATE: A.D. 30   **31-32** 33   47   61

PLACES: Jerusalem: meeting places and homes of the believers

INTRODUCTION

THE CHURCH'S PERSECUTION at the hands of the religionists was its first major test from without. Actually only Peter and John were directly involved, for they were the ones arrested and exposed to the first-degree inquisition of the powerful council. But the entire following of believers knew that the fortunes of their fellowship were at stake; and while Luke does not record it, there must have been much prayer for Peter and John and for the cause of the gospel.

What Luke does record is that the divine help of the Holy Spirit enabled Peter to move from the defensive to the offensive stand by proclaiming the same resurrection truth to the council as he had done to the populace (4:8-12). Peter and John emerged the victors, and the congregation of believers advanced another big step in grace and stature.

98

But—a second test soon reared up, from within. It was the test of *things*. This subject constitutes part of this lesson's study.

PREPARATION FOR STUDY

1) To appreciate fully the situation confronting the young Jewish believers who were forbidden by their rulers to spread the message of Jesus, imagine what would have to be their resources not to be intimidated by the threats. These are Jewish believers, threatened by their own Jewish rulers. This is a totally new experience for them; they have not come this way before. To some there might have been the temptation to remain secret believers. Some may have considered appealing to reverse the council's decision. The shock of it all could have numbed the spiritual life of many. The dark overcast of danger could have upset households prone to explode under extreme tension. Ponder these and other threats to the peace and calm of the early Christian community.

2) Study Psalm 2 and become as familiar with it as were the young Jewish believers who could so easily quote it. Observe especially the context of the first two verses. Read also Exodus 20:11; Nehemiah 9:6; Psalm 146:6; Isaiah 42:5 (cf. Acts 14:15; 17:24).

3) Read Joshua 7 concerning the sin of Achan. Observe especially the real nature of the transgression, the principle determining the judgment, and what the story reveals about God. Some Bible students find many likenesses between the books of Joshua and Acts. The stories of Achan and Ananias certainly are very similar.

ANALYSIS

1) Try reading this passage first in one of the modern English versions, such as Phillips, Williams or Berkeley.

2) The NASB divides this segment into five paragraphs. However, we are suggesting you study the passage in terms of three paragraphs in order to emphasize the three large movements of the narrative.

3) The paragraph 5:1-11 is brought into this segment because

of its natural relation to the previous paragraph, 4:32-37. Notice the common phrase "at the apostles' feet" in 4:35, 37; 5:2.

4) Proceed with your study of the NASB text, reading, observing, making notations in your Bible, and recording textual recreation and topical studies on your analytical chart on page 102.

5) On your chart place the prayer of the first paragraph so it will stand out. Make a thorough study of the outline or logical reasoning of the prayer. In order to understand why the people quoted Psalm 2:1-2, observe this core:

> "Thou who didst make . . .
> didst say, . . . Why?"

The line beginning "Thou who didst make" tells what about God? The lines following "Why" tell what about people and rulers? How does the word "futile" throw light on the "Why" in the core shown?

6) Get in the study habit of identifying the main large content of each paragraph, that is, what each contributes to the progression of the account. Record this in one of the narrow vertical columns. You will find that if this exercise is done early in analysis it will be very helpful in understanding the movement and organization of the biblical text being studied.

7) Notice the word "Christ" in 4:26. Read the NASB marginal note. Compare the quote with the Psalm 2:2 phrase. Relate all this to "anoint" in 4:27.

8) Notice the appearance of the word "Gentiles" in this passage (4:25, 27). What is the significance of this?

9) Observe how the wife Sapphira is shown to have been partner in the false dealing. This reveals something of the active part which the Jewish women played in the life of the Jewish household.

10) Now follow the further suggestions given below the chart on page 102.

11) As you come to the conclusion of your observing and recording, bring together the practical truths taught by the passage.

a) What have you learned about:

Prayer
Faith
Witnessing
Unity of the Believers
Selflessness
Satan, Sin, Judgment

b) Why did God show the signs of 4:31 and 5:5, 10?

c) What do you learn about predestination from the context of 4:28?

d) What do the offerings of this narrative reveal about the early Christians? What were the dangers? What was the significance of laying the offering "at the apostles' feet"?

e) Describe in your own words what was involved in
Being "filled with the Holy Spirit" (4:31)
"Abundant grace . . . upon them" (4:33) (Cf. Luke 2:40)

f) What does 5:9*b* teach about God's revelation given to His people in special instances?

g) What really was the sin of Ananias and Sapphira? What is the impact of Luke's "But"? (5:1). Since all events of the early church are not recorded in Acts, why should this be included? Was the death of Ananias and Sapphira unjust?

h) What is the main timeless universal principle taught in 5:1-11? That is, what truth about sin and judgment revealed here applies to all ages and all people?

i) What kind of fear was it that came upon the whole church? (5:11). (Compare I Peter 1:13-18; Heb. 2:1-3.)

EXPLANATIONS

1) "Joseph" (4:36). A native of the island of Cyprus, Joseph had relatives in Jerusalem (see Acts 12:12 and Col. 4:10). The regulations of Numbers 18:20 and Deuteronomy 10:9 concerning Levites owning property apparently did not apply at this late date. The Levites functioned in the temple in the rather menial tasks of the services.

2) "Ananias . . . Sapphira" (5:1). The name "Ananias" was derived from the Hebrew *Hananiah* ("Jehovah has graciously given"). "Sapphira" is traced back to the Aramaic *shappira*

Acts 4:23—5:11

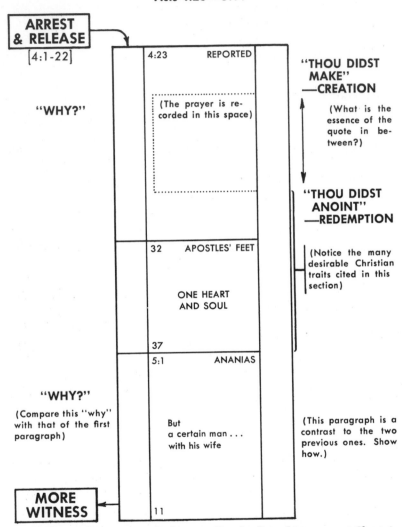

1. Make a study of "The Christian Fellowship" in this passage. Show in the margin what each paragraph contributes to the subject.
2. Study the subject "words" in the first paragraph.
3. Note the Law of Reaping here: second paragraph as related to the first; and last part of third paragraph the consequence of the first part.
4. Study the sequence Faith—Grace—Fear from paragraph to paragraph.
5. Note how the atmosphere changes throughout the passage.

("beautiful"). There is nothing in the account to indicate that these two were not believers.

3) "Satan" (5:3). The English transliterates the Greek *Satanas*, which in turn transliterated the Hebrew common noun *satan*. This Hebrew word meant "adversary" (I Kings 11:14; Ps. 109:6), and was a fitting word for the Greeks to borrow and assign to the evil one, as spiritual adversary of man.

4) "They buried him" (5:6). Undelayed burial was the required practice in Jerusalem.

5) "Church" (5:11). This is the first occurrence in Acts of the Greek word *ekklesía* ("that which is called out"). In secular usage the word was of the vocabulary of Greek democracy, referring to the "popular assembly gathered under its executive officers for the debate and discussion of the State's business."[1] As applied by the people of God to their own religious assembly, the word itself cannot be said to be a distinctively New Testament word, since the Greek translators of the Old Testament (LXX) used *ekklesía* to translate the Hebrew *qahal* ("assembly") at all places except in Genesis, Exodus, Leviticus, Numbers, Jeremiah and Ezekiel. It must be noted however that whenever *qahal* was so translated by *ekklesía* it always referred to a meeting of people in one particular locality, never in the sense of a mystic company of believers.[2]

The word *ekklesía* appears in one hundred and eleven New Testament verses.[3] There are three senses in which it is used: (1) the ideal sense, with reference to the mystic body of Christ, composed of all believers of the New Testament age[4] (e.g., Matt. 16:18; Eph. 1:22); (2) the general contemporary sense, with reference to the world-wide community of believers living at one time (e.g., Acts 9:31); and (3) the purely local sense, designating a group of believers meeting in a particular location (e.g., Acts 11:22).

[1] E. M. Blaiklock, *The Acts of the Apostles* (Grand Rapids: Wm. B. Eerdmans Publishing Co., 1959), p. 73.
[2] See John F. Walvoord, *The Church in Prophecy* (Grand Rapids: Zondervan Publishing House, 1964), p. 18.
[3] The distribution is this: Gospels, 2 verses; Acts, 23; Epistles, 67: Revelation, 19.
[4] This is the premillennial view. The amillennial view interprets "church" to refer to believers of the Old Testament age as well.

Though the word "church" was not new to the people of God, the church of Jesus in the days of Acts was a unique generation of His redeemed ones, entering into a new kind of fellowship as of Pentecost Day, and experiencing a relationship to Jesus and the Holy Spirit which believers before them had not experienced. It was old in the sense in which "it was the continuation and successor of the old 'congregation of Jehovah' which had formerly been confined within the limit of one nation but was now to be thrown open to all believers without distinction."[5]

FURTHER ADVANCED STUDY

1) With the help of an exhaustive concordance, study the references to Satan in the Bible. Satan is referred to in the Bible by many other names and titles. Secure these from a theology book or Bible encyclopedia, and study the Bible's references to them as a supplement to your study of Satan.

If you wish to do further outside reading on this subject, these books are recommended: *The Invisible War*, Donald Grey Barnhouse; *Satan*, Edward M. Bounds; *The Holy War*, John Bunyan; *Satan*, Lewis Sperry Chafer; *Quiet Talks About the Tempter*, S. D. Gordon; *Between God and Satan*, Helmut Thielicke.

2) Study the doctrine of the church. Include in your study these appearances of *ekklesia* in Acts 5:11; 7:38; 8:1, 3; 9:31; 11:22, 26; 12:1, 5; 13:1; 14:23, 27; 15:3-4, 22, 41; 16:5; 18:22; 19:32, 39, 41; 20:17, 28.

Suggested outside readings on the church are: *International Standard Bible Encyclopaedia*, pp. 650-55; *Dispensationalism Today*, Charles Ryrie; *The Supreme Task of the Church*, John T. Seamands; *The Church in Prophecy*, John F. Walvoord. As listed in an earlier lesson, Oswald T. Allis' book *Prophecy and the Church* represents the amillennial viewpoint of this subject.

WORDS TO PONDER

"And when they had been released, *they went to their own* [companions]" (4:23).

---

[5]F. F. Bruce, *Commentary on the Book of Acts* (Grand Rapids: Wm. B. Eerdmans Publishing Co., 1954), p. 116.

LESSON 8

THE TEST OF FORTITUDE

5:12-42

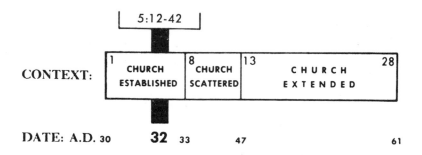

CONTEXT:

DATE: A.D. 30   **32** 33   47   61

PLACES: Jerusalem: Solomon's portico; public jail, council building

INTRODUCTION

THE SHOCKING LOSS of Ananias and Sapphira and the great fear which their execution by God brought upon the whole church did not hinder the apostles from returning to the task of their divine calling. In fact, the momentum of their evangelistic witness kept on accelerating to remarkable proportions, as the passage of this lesson indicates.

Even as God encouraged Joshua, the shamed and despondent general of Israel's army, to banish all fears and return to fight the foe at whose hands he had just suffered an ignoble defeat (Joshua 8:1-2), so God must have driven out of the apostles' hearts any fears and hesitations which would have hindered their continuing ministry. To continue to witness to a mob intent on slaying them surely demanded the utmost of faith and fortitude from the apostles. This was their test of the next weeks.

105

PREPARATION FOR STUDY

Ponder the state of affairs existing in Jerusalem at the end of the passage of the last lesson. It could hardly have been more complex, and the future more unpredictable. Consider these things:

1) The fear over Ananias' and Sapphira's death. Think of the self-examination going on in the believers' hearts, and the care concerning yielding to temptations to sin.

2) The signs and wonders taking place. Could the apostles have been concerned lest the need of spiritual healing be over-shadowed by the physical need? What about the curious? Would the apostles have remembered that multitudes also followed Jesus only out of curiosity?

3) The disruption of the daily routines of life—public and private. How flexible were the household schedules and work routines? Did the new believers think that Jesus might return at any moment?

4) The demands on the physical strength of the apostles. Was there a breaking point? Did they have or need wisdom to budget and control their activities? Could zeal degenerate to fanaticism?

5) The relationship to the religious rulers. Actually the apostles were under a ban, at liberty only on probation. How would they maintain a right heart by disobeying the ban? What about their love to their enemies?

6) The appearance of new faces from outside Jerusalem. Might the apostles have thought: Will this thing spread to other cities, even to other lands? Considering the fact that thousands had already believed, might there have been any action on the part of the apostles to initiate some form of organization, to encourage a follow-up program of order, efficiency and development?

Let the above questions suggest what might have been some of the problems and situations confronting the Jerusalem church at this time.

ANALYSIS

1) As the chart on page 109 shows, the paragraph divisions

of NASB are followed with the exception that an additional paragraph is begun at 5:27. Mark this addition in your Bible.

2) Read through the passage, keeping the four paragraphs in mind. In your first reading you should always identify any block of material, such as a quote from the Old Testament or an extended discourse by a person in the narrative. Observe two such units in this segment. Block them off in your Bible and on your analytical chart on page 109.

3) This segment is longer than what one can substantially reproduce on his analytical chart in terms of textual re-creation. In recording your textual re-creation, print only the more significant words and phrases. Use dots (. . . or . . . .) to indicate your omissions.

4) Keep on developing your eye to observe. This is one facet of the Bible study process in which you should develop keenness. What things should be observed? Every passage is different, but subconsciously you should be on the lookout for such items as repetitions, key words and phrases, strong words, cores of long sentences, turning points, pungent statements of doctrine, implied subsurface truths, comparisons and contrasts, progressions, amplifications, atmospheres, relations, actions, persons, places, etc. These are the things which you should record on your analytical chart, either in the margins or in the textual re-creation within the paragraph boxes.

5) Notice the oft-repeated word "but" in this segment. Follow through the study of the following three appearances of "but" in the context, recording your study on your chart:

"Filled with jealousy"	(17)
"but"	(19)
"We gave you strict orders"	(28)
"but"	(29)
"Intending to slay them"	(33)
"but"	(34)

Pursue this study of "but" further, on your own.

6) Compare the logical reasoning of Peter and Gamaliel. Who is the central person of Gamaliel's argument? Of Peter's?

7) In Peter's message, start with the object "Jesus-Prince-Saviour," and note all the words Peter relates to Him.

8) Study the word "all" in this segment.

9) Continue your analysis by pursuing the lines of study suggested below the accompanying chart.

10) Coming now to the last stages of your study, answer the following on the basis of what this passage teaches:

- a) Note the three relationships mentioned in 5:12-13. What is taught here?

- b) The "point of contact" of healing in verse 15 was Peter's shadow. Was a point of contact necessary? Justify your answer.

- c) What does verse 20 contribute to your understanding of where the apostles got their boldness to speak, despite being under a ban?

- d) What is the real compulsion of Peter's "We *must* obey God"? (5:29). Does he cite God's authority or power? In what sense does the phrase "forgiveness of sins" (5:31) explain the "must"?

- e) Describe the "rejoicing" of 5:41. Compare this with the "rejoicing" of 8:39 (same Greek word, *chairō*). What is the common ingredient of each? Read the following verses in connection with the ministry of suffering for Jesus' name: Matthew 10:17ff; Mark 13:9ff; Luke 12:11-12; 21:12ff; John 15:18ff; 16:2ff; I Peter 4:14, 16.

- f) List ten important lessons on witnessing which this passage teaches.

EXPLANATIONS

1) "Solomon's portico" (5:12). The new fellowship of believers had continued to meet together in the temple from the very first day of their common life at Pentecost (see 2:46), and by this time they had established a regular pattern of Christian public worship, apart from any participation they may have had in the temple services. Not having a building of their own, it was very convenient to meet in the courts of the temple area. Solomon's

WHEN GOD IS IN THE PLANS
Acts 5:12-42

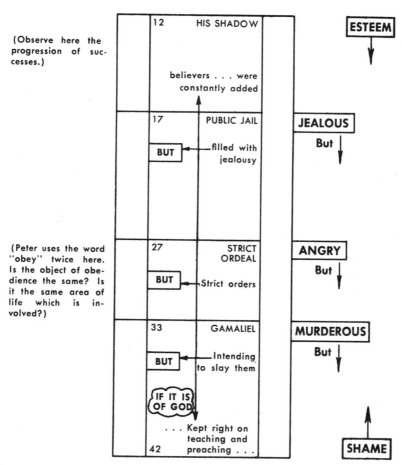

(Observe here the progression of successes.)

12   HIS SHADOW

ESTEEM

believers . . . were constantly added

17   PUBLIC JAIL

JEALOUS
But

BUT — filled with jealousy

(Peter uses the word "obey" twice here. Is the object of obedience the same? Is it the same area of life which is involved?)

27   STRICT ORDEAL

ANGRY
But

BUT — Strict orders

33   GAMALIEL

MURDEROUS
But

BUT — Intending to slay them

IF IT IS OF GOD

. . . Kept right on teaching and
42   preaching . . .

SHAME

1. Use the left narrow vertical column for indicating main content of each paragraph; the right column for any grouping of large subject matter.
2. Make a study of the progression of the opposition's attitude of mind, beginning with "jealousy" (v. 17).
3. Compare the beginning and end of the segment.
4. Note the words "esteem" and "shame." Pursue this study further.
5. Observe the signs of the rulers' impotency in the passage.
6. Make a study of "witness" as this subject appears in each paragraph.
7. Starting with the key center "If it is of God," develop the topic "When God Is in the Plans" from paragraph to paragraph.

portico was evidently the usual place of assembly. Refer again
to the temple area diagram (p. 87) to visualize the setting.

2) "Cities in the vicinity of Jerusalem" (5:16). Consult a map
of the environs of Jerusalem in New Testament days to acquaint
yourself with these numerous suburb towns.

3) "Public jail" (5:18). This was different from the ward to
which Peter and John had been earlier assigned. Apparently all
the leading apostles were jailed on this occasion.

4) "Senate" (5:21). The intent of the "and" is explicative, the
meaning being, "they called the Council together, and [that is]
all the Senate of the Children of Israel, . . ."

5) "Gamaliel" (5:34). Gamaliel was a spokesman for the
strong and influential minority of Pharisees which belonged to
the council. Once a disciple of Hillel, he now was leader of the
school of Hillel, which claimed many keen disciples, including
Saul of Tarsus (see 22:3). One of his official titles was "Rabban
Gamaliel the Elder." Gamaliel was unquestionably the most respected Jewish teacher of his day.

6) "Flogged" (5:40). This probably was the common torture
of thirty-nine stripes (read Deut. 25:3 and II Cor. 11:24).

FURTHER ADVANCED STUDY

1) With the help of an exhaustive concordance, make a topical
study of the subject "repentance" as taught in Acts; extend your
study also to what the remainder of the New Testament teaches.

2) Examine the soundness of Gamaliel's advice. Are there any
flaws here? Did he say enough? If Paul was one of Gamaliel's
disciples, why did Paul later persecute the church?

WORDS TO PONDER

"Speak . . . the whole message of this Life" (5:20).

THE TEST OF RESPONSIBILITY

6:1-15

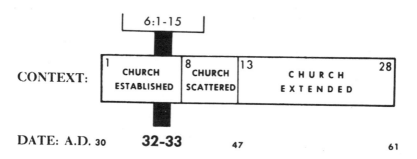

CONTEXT:

1 CHURCH ESTABLISHED	8 CHURCH SCATTERED	13 CHURCH EXTENDED 28

DATE: A.D. 30   **32-33**   47   61

PLACES: Jerusalem: meeting place of the believers; council chamber

INTRODUCTION

WHATEVER EXPERIENCES the church passed through in its infancy years, it always seemed to emerge larger, stronger and more mature. Luke's narrative of Acts 3-7 teaches this very clearly, as the summary on page 112 indicates.

The church's growth was not confined to its infancy stage however. At intervals along the way in Acts (approximately five years between each point) Luke makes a special note of the church's progress. Read what Luke says in these verses: 9:31; 12:24; 16:5; 19:20; 28:31.

Luke's purpose in Acts 6 is twofold: (1) to record another internal problem of the early church, and (2) to introduce Stephen as the focal point of the more intense persecution which ensued against the church (cf. 8:1*b*).

	3:1-26	4:1-22	5:1-16	5:17-42	6:1-7	6:8—8:1a
ACTIVITY OR PROBLEM	—lame man healed —Peter preaches	**EXTERNAL PROBLEM** Peter and John —arrested —tried —released	**INTERNAL PROBLEM** sin in midst	**EXTERNAL PROBLEM** apostles —jailed —tried —released	**INTERNAL PROBLEM** —schism —complaint problem solved	**EXTERNAL PROBLEM** Stephen apprehended
		→ number of believers up to 5,000 men	→ —awe —unity —believers constantly added —surrounding cities attracted	→ apostles continue teaching, preaching. disciples increasing in number	→ number of disciples increasing many priests converted	**8:1b ff.**
REFERENCE TO GROWTH		**4:23-37** Prayer and praise of the fellowship —unity —power —grace —boldness to witness				→ believers scattered, preaching the Word (8:1b ff.)

PREPARATION FOR STUDY

1) Review the analyses of Acts which you have made thus far. Construct your own outline of the progress of Luke's account through chapter 7. (Though you have not analyzed chapter 7 as yet, it will not be difficult for you to see its place in the narrative.)

2) It is well to be reminded again that while all the evangelistic activity and congregating for worship were going on day by day, the believers also had their daily chores to do and problems to meet. Try to visualize the many kinds of problems and temptations that faced the early Christians—individually and corporately.

One situation existed which had the potential of dividing the early church. For a few centuries the Jewish world had had two "types" of Jews:[1] *Hebrews* who spoke Aramaic and most of whom were natives of Palestine; and *Hellenists*[2] who, though born Jews, usually spoke Greek and assimilated much of the Greek culture, and by birth or another means had some close connection with a foreign Greek land. The natural nationalistic barrier between the two groups eventually reared itself even in the midst of the thriving group of Jewish believers, as is indicated by this passage.

3) Consider also the problems which faced the early church: mass evangelism and worship by an exceedingly large multitude. Is there a premium to be placed on order, organization, efficiency? Observe Jesus' ways with 5,000 men plus women and children (read Mark 6:35-44).

ANALYSIS

1) Set up your analytical chart to show the two paragraphs indicated on the chart on page 114. (You may choose to follow the NASB and make verse 7 a paragraph by itself.) In deriving a main topical study, you should look for at least three main points, even though you may be showing just two paragraphs.

2) After a careful reading of the chapter, continue with all the procedures of analytical study. As to recording, remember that "the pencil is one of the best eyes."

3) As in previous segments of Acts, there are blocks of discourse here. Show the blocks clearly on your analytical chart.

[1]There were of course a small number of proselytes to the Jewish faith. But the two groups cited here represent those who were born Jews.
[2]The word *Hellenist* comes from the Greek *hēllēnizō*, "to speak Greek."

Acts 6:1-15

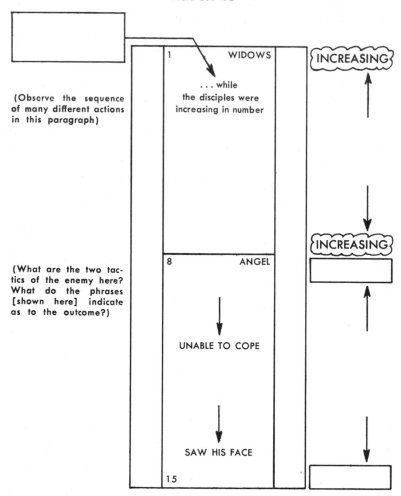

1. Relate 6:1 to what had just been recorded in Acts. Observe the references to "increase" at the beginning and end of paragraph 6:1-7. Identify by one word the intervening contents of the paragraph.
2. Relate the beginning of paragraph 6:8-15 to the end, and show what comes between.
3. Study the two basic aspects of "truth" and "falsehood." Show how these appear throughout the segment.
4. Record on your chart the various atmospheres.
5. Record in the margins the various descriptions of Stephen.
6. Look for contrasts in the segment.

4) The two paragraphs reveal two entirely different kinds of problems. Record these in one of the side vertical columns. Use the other column for a more detailed outline of the segment.

5) Now follow the suggestions for analysis shown below the accompanying chart.

6) There are many vital lessons to be learned from this passage. Consider the following aspects:

a) The schism between the Hellenistic (Greek) Jews and the native Hebrews was apparently over just this one problem. What happens to schism when not nipped in the bud?

b) Did the twelve scorn the task of serving tables? Why were the spiritual qualifications so strict for men filling this vacant office? What were the three areas of the qualifications?

c) What were the two areas of ministry which the apostles dared not neglect? Make present-day applications.

d) The names of the seven chosen all appear to be Greek names. Relate this to the original complaint and the unanimous approval.

e) What is the impact of the terms "kept on" and "continued" in 6:7?

f) Notice the details of the false accusations recorded in verses 11-14. What was the purpose of such lies?

g) "They were unable to cope with the wisdom and the Spirit with which he was speaking" (v. 10). What was involved in such speaking?

h) To what extent was the second tactic of false accusation successful? Can falsehood be combated? If so, how?

i) What marks of strong Christian character are revealed in this passage?

EXPLANATIONS

1) "While the disciples were increasing" (6:1). This is the first of twenty-eight appearances of the word "disciple" (Greek *mathētēs*) in Acts. It is found in the Synoptics one hundred sixty times; in John, seventy-eight times, and nowhere else in the New Testament. It seems that the further the church moved in time

from the earthly ministry of Jesus, the more the word "disciples" was replaced by other designations, such as "brethren" and "saints," which are two of the most common titles for them in the epistles. Try to explain this change, remembering that the word itself literally means "a taught one," and referred most often in the New Testament to those taught by Christ.

2) "Their widows were being overlooked" (6:1). For some reason it was the Hellenistic widows who were overlooked. Luke does not give an explanation.[3]

3) "Stephen . . ." (6:5). All seven names are Greek. Only Stephen and Philip play an important part in the story of Acts.

4) "They laid their hands on them" (6:6). Compare Numbers 27:23; Acts 8:17; 9:12, 17; 19:6.

5) "Many of the priests were becoming obedient" (6:7). These were the ordinary priests, not the members of the chief-priest families which were the instigators of opposition to the apostles.

6) "Synagogue of the Freedmen" (6:9). This was one of the many synagogues in Jerusalem. It was attended by Jews who came from lands of the dispersions: Cyrene and Alexandria of Africa, and Cilicia and Asia to the north. Paul, whose home was Tarsus of Cilicia, could very well have been among this group.

7) "We have heard him say that . . . Jesus will destroy" (6:14). Compare John 2:19; Mark 14:58; Matthew 26:61.

FURTHER ADVANCED STUDY

1) It should be obvious after reading this much of the book of Acts that the fullness of the Holy Spirit in the lives of the apostles and laymen of the early church was the key to their spiritual vitality and fruitfulness. An important topical study for Acts is on the subject of the Holy Spirit. In making such a study, the scope of the project may be kept broad, including all phases of the Holy Spirit's person and work, or confined to such an area as the Spirit's fullness. Be sure to let the context of each of Acts' references do its valuable interpretive service.

You also may want to extend your study of the topic of the Holy Spirit to other parts of the New Testament, especially the epistles.

[3]One early manuscript adds this phrase at the end of the verse: "because it was being administered by Hebrews."

Such a study would include, for example, such verses as Ephesians 5:18, which clearly indicates through a contrasting figure what is behind the *picture* word "filled."

For outside reading on the Holy Spirit here are some suggested sources: *The Holy Spirit*, Wick Broomall; *The Work of the Holy Spirit*, Abraham Kuyper; *Spirit of the Living God*, Leon Morris; *The Holy Spirit: His Gifts and Power*, John Owen; *The Person and Work of the Holy Spirit*, Rene Pache; *The Witness of the Spirit*, Bernard Ramm; *The Holy Spirit in the New Testament*, Henry Barclay Swete; *The Holy Spirit of God*, Wm. H. Griffith Thomas; *The Holy Spirit*, Reuben A. Torrey; *The Holy Spirit*, John F. Walvoord.

2) Study the word "wisdom" (*sophia*) as it appears in the New Testament. Use a concordance to direct you to the verses.

WORDS TO PONDER
"The word of God kept on spreading" (6:7).

THE TEST OF GRACE

7:1–8:1a

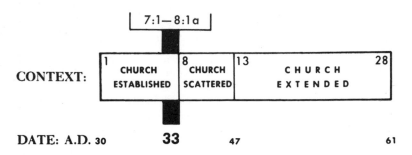

CONTEXT:

1 CHURCH ESTABLISHED	8 CHURCH SCATTERED	13 CHURCH EXTENDED 28

DATE: A.D. 30   **33**   47   61

PLACE: Jerusalem: council chamber

RULERS: Caiaphas, Pontius Pilate

INTRODUCTION

IN THE LARGE MOVEMENT of the story of Acts, chapter 7 serves as a transitional chapter. It relates to what has gone before, for Stephen was one of the seven Spirit-filled men chosen to serve over the problem of the widows, as recorded in chapter 6. But it also relates to what follows, for the slaying of Stephen, recorded at the end of chapter 7, sets in motion a full-fledged organized persecution against the church, which Luke begins to record at 8:1b.[1] It is rather arbitrary, therefore, where one places chapter 7 in the survey of Acts, whether as part of the section "Church Established" (chaps. 1–7), or of the section "Church Scattered"

---

[1]Stephen may also be seen as a forerunner of Paul, especially as to the message he preached. Blaiklock remarks, "by his teaching Stephen broke the ground for Paul's universalism." E. M. Blaiklock, *The Acts of the Apostles* (Grand Rapids: Wm. B. Eerdmans Publishing Co., 1959), p. 76.

(chaps. 7–12). The outline of this manual follows the former association.

Because of its length,[2] it is recommended that the segment 7:1–8:1a be analyzed in two units. Actually, then, this Lesson 10 contains two study lessons. In order to afford variety in the study, the two units will be treated differently, with more independent study required in the second unit. The division of the text of Acts into the two study units is as follows:

7:1	7:2	7:51	7:54 8:1a
INTRODUCTION	STEPHEN'S DEFENSE		EFFECT
	BASIS OF THE DEFENSE	APPLICATION	
UNIT 1 ISRAEL'S YESTERDAY "your fathers did" 7:51		UNIT 2 ISRAEL'S TODAY "you are doing" 7:51	

If one word can spell out the life and ministry of Jesus, it is the word "grace." Grace was manifested to the very end by Jesus when He cried out from the cross, "Father, forgive them; for they do not know what they are doing" (Luke 23:34). It was to be a test throughout the ages on how the church would react on seeing the Lord's grace rejected by the ones for whom He died. Stephen's reactions reflected the spirit of Jesus, even as he pleaded the Lord's forgiveness for his murderers with his last breath.

I. UNIT ONE: ISRAEL'S YESTERDAY (7:1-50)

The Jews revered their heritage even though they were not living in the light of it. To them, the promises, the law, the tabernacle and temple, the patriarchs, kings and prophets, the land of

[2]Chapter 7 is the longest chapter of Acts. The average number of verses in the chapters of Acts, is thirty-nine. The range is from fifteen to sixty.

their fathers and the city of Zion, *were their religion.* Therefore, the false charges leveled against Stephen dealt explicitly with some of these. This was Stephen's grand opportunity to reveal the truth of Israel's yesterday, and show how Israel up to that time had not changed: "You are doing [Israel's today] just as your fathers did [Israel's yesterday]" (7:51*b*).

Before reading the highlights of Israel's past history which Stephen selected out of the hosts of experiences which were theirs, review in your own mind the eras of that history as given by the Old Testament record. Use the following chart as a help:

1,500 YEARS OF JEWISH HISTORY

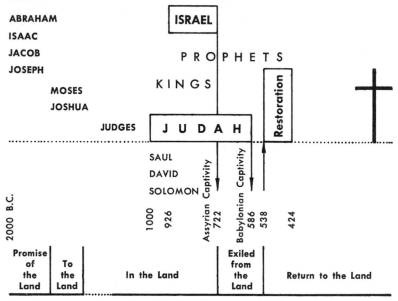

After you have reviewed the history of Israel, refer to the text of Stephen's address. Before reading, make paragraph divisions in the text at verses 2, 8*b* ("and Isaac"), 20, 30, 35, 44. Read the entire segment at one time, underlining or noting those words or phrases that stand out in this reading.

Study the chart shown on page 122 which suggests various outlines of the material which Stephen cited in his thumbnail historical sketch. Some key phrases also have been included in the chart, but you are encouraged to look for more, and list them on a similar chart of your own. The purpose of this method of visual aids in study is always to be able to see the parts in relation to the whole, and also to be able to recognize the multiplicity of ideas which Stephen was developing simultaneously as he was speaking.

After you have studied the chart, follow these suggestions for study of the biblical text:

1) Observe the different aspects of the bright picture of Israel's history in the first two paragraphs (2-19). Contrast this with the Moses era (20-43). How does the paragraph 7:35-43 end? What was Stephen trying to get across in all of this?

2) 7:39. Why is this such a strong indictment against Israel? Relate this to 7:51-53.

3) 7:44-50. What is the one subject here? Who are the four men mentioned in 44-47? Which words used here refer to a place of worship? For background to your study of 7:44-50, consult Bible dictionaries and other books for the underlying purposes and pedagogy of God's tabernacle and God's house. In the Bible read Exodus 24:12–31:18 (note especially 25:8); 35:1–39:43; II Samuel 7:1-16; I Kings 8:1-43; Psalm 132:2-5.

SOME APPLICATIONS

Because of the variety of experiences which comprise the history of Israel, various applications can be derived from this passage. Consider the following:

1) What is learned here about the call of God to His servants?
2) What does the passage teach about:

> faith; promises of God
> trials by God
> persecution; rejection
> judgment
> gospel for all
> grace; long-suffering of God
> worship

3) Notice (by the NASB capitalizations) how frequently Stephen quoted the Old Testament in his historical survey.

STEPHEN'S REHEARSAL OF ISRAEL'S PAST
Acts 7:2-50

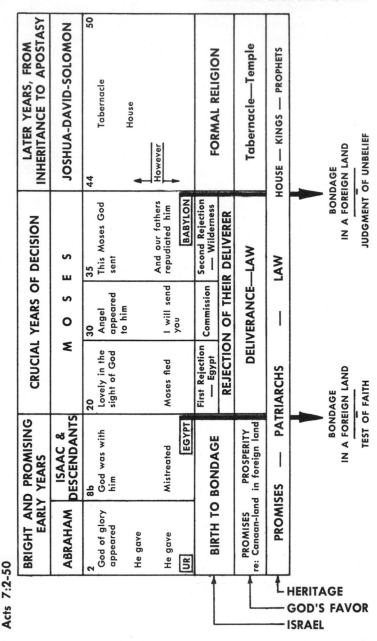

4) "The place on which you are standing is holy ground" (7:33). Note other places in the text that might be described as holy ground. What makes a place "holy ground"?

5) Make a list of all the geographical places cited by Stephen, citing spiritual lessons out of Israel's history which are suggested by many of them.

EXPLANATIONS

1) "The high priest" (7:1). Caiaphas was probably the presiding high priest of the council at this time. It was Caiaphas before whom Jesus was brought on trial for charges similar to Stephen's. Think about what may have been going through his mind, even as he spoke such caustic words as: "Are these things so?" (7:1).

2) "Covenant of circumcision" (7:8). Circumcision was a rite practiced by many heathen nations, but it was given a unique spiritual meaning for the Israelites in that it symbolized the covenant between God and Israel (Rom. 4:11). Read Genesis 17:9-14 for its first appearance as a religious rite for Israel.

3) "Moloch . . . Rompha" (7:42-43). These were planetary gods, part of the "host of heaven" referred to in 7:42.[3]

II. UNIT TWO: ISRAEL'S TODAY (7:51—8:1a)

Though Stephen was undoubtedly aware of the severity of the consequences which might be aroused by his address about Israel's Yesterday and Israel's Today, he could not have had a more advantageous situation for such an address. First, the council was hypnotized, as it were, to give him their utmost attention. For fixing their gaze on him, they "saw his face like the face of an angel" (6:15). Then, Stephen was speaking on invitation from the high priest. Furthermore, most of Stephen's address to the council was purely historical, based on true facts which his educated hearers could not deny. Another advantage Stephen had

[3]Bruce writes of this, "It was more particularly under the Assyrian influence in the eighth century B.C. that the worship of the planetary divinities became so popular in Israel, but the evidence of Canaanite place-names shows that they were worshipped as early as the period of the Tell el-Amarna correspondence (c. 1370 B.C.)." F. F. Bruce, *Commentary on the Book of Acts* (Grand Rapids: Wm. B. Eerdmans Publishing Co., 1954), p. 156.

was that he did not speak as an outsider. He did not deny being descended from those who repudiated Moses, for example. They were "our" fathers, he said. And to impress even further his own identification with his hearers, he addressed the gathering with the intimate "brethren" and "fathers"[4] (7:2).

After reviewing the pertinent highlights of Israel's Yesterday, Stephen did not need to say much more, because the historical events he cited proved his point. But the moment of truth had now arrived when he must get personal and point his finger at the guilty souls of his hearers. The "our fathers" suddenly became "your fathers" (7:51), not because Stephen now deserted the family, but because he was no longer a party with them in their sin. Stephen was a redeemed one, *saved from* the perverse generation about which Peter preached on Pentecost Day (cf. 2:40).

ANALYSIS

Proceed with your own analysis of 7:51–8:1a on the basis of the background of the segment already studied. Feel free to use any of the methods of study already suggested by this manual, or to apply some adaptations or procedures of your own. (Flexibility and adaptability are valuable assets for the Bible student.)

At the conclusion of your analysis, write out some of the truths taught by this segment about obedience, resisting the Holy Spirit, grace, long-suffering, the sinful heart, forgiveness, rewards of the righteous.

EXPLANATIONS

1) "The law as ordained by angels" (7:53). Compare Galatians 3:19 and Hebrews 2:2.

2) "Son of Man" (7:56). The title "Son of Man" was Jesus' favorite reference to Himself. This is the only place in the New Testament where it is spoken of Him by anyone else (the phrases of Rev. 1:13 and 14:14 are not the same as this title). What great truths are inherent in the expression?

[4]Marvin R. Vincent identifies the "brethren" as the audience in general, and the "fathers" as the members of the Sanhedrin. *Word Studies in the New Testament*, Vol. I (Grand Rapids: Wm. B. Eerdmans Publishing Co., 1946), p. 477.

3) "Standing at the right hand of God" (7:56). What is significant about this statement, in the light of these verses: Psalm 110:1; Ephesians 1:20; Colossians 3:1; Hebrews 1:3, 13?

4) "Stoning" (7:58). The violence of the mob action suggests that this was a lynching without the sanction of the council. But the fact that witnesses functioned at the stoning (apparently according to the law prescribed in Leviticus 24:14, 16 and Deuteronomy 17:7; of I Kings 21:10) makes it appear that the council gave the verdict of blasphemy. There is no reference to Stephen's case being brought before the governor Pontius Pilate for review, which was required by law.

5) "The witnesses laid aside their robes" (7:58). The witnesses took off their robes so that they could throw the first stones. Of the procedure of stoning, Vincent writes:

> According to the Rabbis, the scaffold to which the criminal was to be led, with his hands bound, was to be twice the size of a man. One of the witnesses was to smite him with a stone upon the breast, so as to throw him down. If he were not killed, the second witness was to throw another stone at him. Then, if he were yet alive, all the people were to stone him until he was dead. The body was then to be suspended till sunset.[5]

6) "A young man named Saul" (7:58). This, together with 8:1a, is Paul's introduction to Luke's narrative. The expression "young man" does not identify Paul's age, for it could refer to someone as old as forty-five years. As noted in an earlier chapter, Paul at this time was no doubt a leader in one of the synagogues of Jerusalem. Perhaps he was not a member of the council at this time, but this cannot be determined. Concerning "these men," he did not follow the advice of his teacher Gamaliel to "let them alone" (5:38); instead, he was wholeheartedly for the stoning of Stephen, "watching out for the cloaks of those who were slaying him" (22:20). It was an hour he would never forget—nor would God *let* him forget it.

FURTHER ADVANCED STUDY

1) Study the subject "Israel and the Judgments of God,"

[5]Vincent, *op. cit.*, pp. 485-86. Vincent's description would probably not fit too closely those stonings where riot, not order, was the scene.

especially with reference to Old Testament history. The message of prophets like Jeremiah will shed much light on this.

2) Stephen was a noble example of grace. The word "grace" appears ten times in Acts. Beginning with what you learn of grace (directly or indirectly) from this lesson, and proceeding to the other references of Acts, formulate a list of the various aspects of this attribute.

WORDS TO PONDER

"I see the heavens opened up" (7:56).

SAMARITANS SAVED

8:1b-25

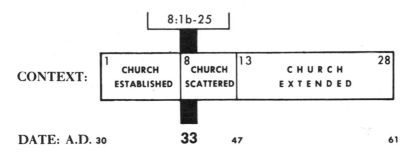

8:1b-25

CONTEXT:

1 CHURCH ESTABLISHED	8 CHURCH SCATTERED	13 CHURCH EXTENDED 28

DATE: A.D. 30   **33**   47   61

PLACES: City of Samaria; villages of the region of Samaria

RULERS: Caiaphas, Pontius Pilate

INTRODUCTION

WITH THE DEATH of Stephen was born a new era for the church. Although it was healthy and virile, it was not without new problems and more extensive persecution. God's design now called for an advance and multiplication of the church in two ways: geographically, from the city of Jerusalem to the villages of Judea and Samaria; and nationally, from the particularism of the elect nation of Israel, to the universalism of the people of all nations—represented in the New Testament as the Gentiles. The time was ripe for the fulfillment of Simeon's expectation of Gentile salvation uttered about forty years earlier,

> "Mine eyes have seen Thy salvation,
> Which Thou hast prepared in the presence of all peoples,
> a light of revelation to the Gentiles . . . ."
>
> (Luke 2:30-32a).

127

So the blood of Stephen was seed literally scattered upon the fertile fields of neighboring lands, and the fruit thereof was good and abundant.

The years described by Acts 8—12 were transitional years for the church's history. During this time the apostles first accepted the fact that the gospel was for the Gentile as well as for the Jew, and with this their foreign missions outlook was born. Peter begins to leave Luke's narrative as Paul is brought into the story in anticipation of the westward thrust of the church's program which he is to lead. If Luke's designed terminus for the story of Acts was an apostle's setting foot on the soil of Rome, then chapter 13 begins the advance to that city, and the section Acts 8—12 shows the preparatory stages for that advance.

The accompanying chart shows some of the main setting and contents of Acts 8—12. For comparative purposes, the survey also includes Acts 1—7. Refer to your own survey of Acts for review.

Acts 1—12

1	3	6	8:1b	9:32			12
JERUSALEM			JUDEA and SAMARIA				
CHURCH ESTABLISHED			CHURCH SCATTERED				
CHURCH IS BORN	CHURCH GROWS THROUGH TESTING		CHURCH IS SCATTERED	CHURCH EMBRACES GENTILES			
PETER and JOHN		STEPHEN	PAUL ————————————→ P E T E R PHILIP - BARNABAS ——————→				
A.D. 30 ABOUT 3 YEARS			A.D. 33 ABOUT 13 YEARS A.D. 46				

PREPARATION FOR STUDY

1) Refer to the map on page 131 which shows the areas and movements of the apostolic work described by Luke in Acts 8—12. Fix in your mind the locations of cities visited and routes taken.

2) This passage describes the first ministry of the gospel to the Samaritans. Recall the geography of Jesus' commission of 1:8. The apostles were not told the manner nor the time of the advance of their witness beyond Jerusalem. If they ever speculated about this, what might have been some of their thoughts?

3) You should be acquainted with the Samaritans' religious history in regard to its relationship to the Jews in order to appreciate the barrier which was now about to be broken down by the church.

Samaritans' History

a) North-south rivalry originated in the cleavage between the northern kingdom of Israel and the southern kingdom of Judah (c. 930 B.C.).

b) Israel was taken captive by Sargon II of Assyria in 722 B.C. A remnant of the poorer class were left behind to till the soil. (II Kings 17).

c) Pagan foreigners were imported into the land by Sargon to replace the deportees. Intermarriage brought on a new race of people, considered half-breeds in the eyes of pure Jews.

d) When the Jews of Babylon, comprised mainly of descendants of the southern kingdom and partly of remnants of the northern kingdom, returned from their Babylonian captivity in the days of Ezra and Nehemiah (around A.D. 540), the Samaritans offered to help rebuild the temple at Jerusalem.

e) The Jews bluntly refused the offer from those whom they scorned as aliens, and a bitter hostility between the two people ensued.

f) Around 400 B.C. the Samaritans built their own temple on their own holy hill, Mt. Gerizim (cf. John 4:20), and claimed the Pentateuch (with their own changes inserted) as solely theirs. This caused them to be considered heretics and schismatics by all Jews.

g) The Samaritans were later conquered and their temple destroyed by the Hasmonean king John Hyrcanus I (135-104 B.C.); but eventually they regained their freedom from the Jews with the Roman conquest of Palestine.

h) The friction between Samaritans and Jews continued

throughout Jesus' lifetime. Jews traveling between Judea and Galilee commonly went by way of Perea, on the east side of the Jordan, and thus skirted Samaria. Jesus regarded His mission as primarily to the house of Israel, but on occasions He ministered in Samaria (cf. Luke 9:51-56). Just before His ascension He clearly included Samaria in the Great Commission (Acts 1:8).

SAMARITANS' CREED

a) There is one God

b) Moses is His prophet

c) The Pentateuch[1] is His written revelation

d) Mt. Gerizim is the appointed place for sacrifice

e) There is a day of judgment and recompense

f) Moses shall one day return as Taheb, or restorer (cf. John 4:25)

4) On the day that Stephen was stoned it must have been as though all the hosts of darkness were let loose to ravage the believers (especially the Hellenist believers) dwelling in Jerusalem. Previously only the leaders in the Jerusalem church had been apprehended, though all the saints must have sensed what the inevitable outcome would be. The opposition forces still did not have a leader who could personally rally the forces to an organized campaign of relentless fury.

If the Jewish religious rulers had been looking for a leader who would be a personification of wisdom, they would have gone to Gamaliel. But the temporizing policy he recommended scratched him off as a candidate. The Jews' champion had to be a man of zeal—fanatic zeal—and they must have considered themselves fortunate to find such a glowing prospect in Saul of Tarsus. Saul finds his way into Luke's narrative through the back door, as it were, but as soon as he arrives a great persecution arises. This is the explosive quality of zeal, and it was spilled upon the church.

As you read the verses of this passage, try to picture in your own mind how you would feel if you were driven from your home and city for the sake of the gospel.

[1]That is, the Pentateuch as it was radically altered by the Samaritans.

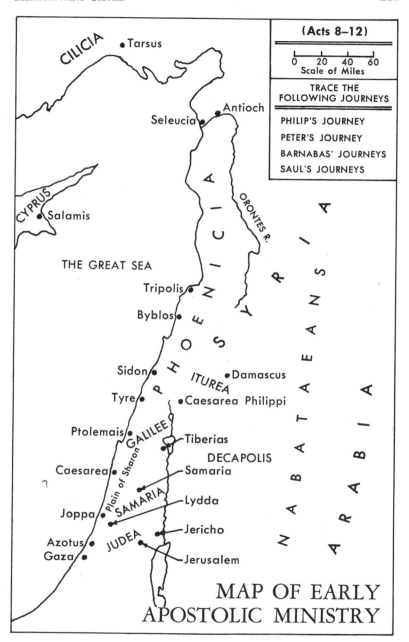

Tarsus

Antioch
Seleucia

CYPRUS
Salamis

S
Y
R
I
A

ORONTES R.

PHOENICIA

THE GREAT SEA

Tripolis

Byblos

Sidon   Damascus
ITUREA
Tyre   Caesarea Philippi

Ptolemais
GALILEE
Tiberias

Caesarea   DECAPOLIS
Plain of Sharon   Samaria

Joppa   SAMARIA   Lydda

Azotus   JUDEA   Jericho
Gaza   Jerusalem

N
A
B
A
T
A
E
A
N
S

A
R
A
B
I
A

(Acts 8–12)

0   20   40   60
Scale of Miles

TRACE THE
FOLLOWING JOURNEYS

PHILIP'S JOURNEY
PETER'S JOURNEY
BARNABAS' JOURNEYS
SAUL'S JOURNEYS

MAP OF EARLY
APOSTOLIC MINISTRY

ANALYSIS

1) For this segment of Acts use the paragraph divisions shown on the accompanying chart (same as NASB). You will note that the last paragraph is just one verse, but in view of its content it stands on its own as a separate paragraph. (In doing a main topical study for your analytical chart, a paragraph point for this last paragraph may be omitted.)

2) Note by the accompanying chart that the first and last paragraphs are set off from the rest of the segment. Why? Your analytical chart should justify such an outline. In what ways is the first paragraph an introduction to the remainder of Acts?

3) Complete the geographical outline started in the narrow left-hand column.

4) Develop further the outline shown: Attention . . . Belief . . .
Receiving

5) Observe the large division of content in the third and fourth paragraphs, each divided into two parts:

(Simon) — (Philip)   ;   (Peter and John) — (Simon).

6) Now follow the suggested studies shown below the accompanying chart.

7) Further interpretations and applications:

a) 8:1b-3. The apostles did not leave Jerusalem. What may have been their reasons? Why would not the persecution have forced them out also? (It is a known fact that for the next one hundred years after this persecution, most of the believers living in Jerusalem were Hebrews, for the Hellenist believers were the ones mainly driven from the holy city.) Where did Saul get his authority to ravage the church? (cf. 26:10). What was his motivation? (cf. Galatians 1:14). Read James 1:1 and I Peter 1:1 for references to believers (probably Jewish) of the dispersion.

b) 8:4-8. What noble example is given in 8:4? What was the cause of the rejoicing of 8:8? What special significance would the miracles of this paragraph have in light of verses 9-11?

Notice that Philip is the key person of this section of Acts. What was Philip's former relation to Stephen? Might this suggest that the persecution of 8:1b was mainly directed to the leaders of the Hellenists?

Acts 8:1b-25

ATMOSPHERE:

	JERUSALEM			CONTRASTS
tumult lamentation		1b RAVAGING		
ATTENTION to the message		4 SAMARIA		
SIMON		9 MAGIC SIMON . . . . PHILIP		
BELIEF in Christ				
RECEIVING of the Holy Spirit		14 GALL PETER and JOHN . . . . SIMON		
		25 VILLAGES		

1. Complete the study of atmosphere throughout the passage. In verse 25 notice the word "solemnly." How does this fit in with the word "gospel," which literally means "glad tidings"? Considering all that had taken place in Samaria, what may be another implied atmosphere for the last paragraph?
2. Study the many contrasts in the third and fourth paragraphs.
3. What does the passage tell about the changes of Simon's heart?
4. Notice references to Jerusalem. What was the church's continued relationship to the holy city?
5. Observe the various ways the ministry of the Word is represented, e.g., "preaching the good news."
6. Notice the appearances of the word "attention" here.

c) 8:9-13. Simon sought greatness. Whom did Philip extol?
Note Luke's reference to "women" in verse 12. This is the fourth
such reference in Acts (read again 1:14; 5:14; 8:3; 8:12). What
has the gospel done for people's respect for women?

d) 8:14-25. Why did the church at Jerusalem send Peter and
John to Samaria? Recall an earlier experience of John in Samaria
(Luke 9:51-56). As the people were receiving the Holy Spirit,
would they have "felt" the experience? Were there external manifestations here? Notice how sharply Peter rebuked Simon's sin.
Compare this sin with that of Ananias. Account for the different
outcomes. Do you think Simon's "believing" of verse 13 was a
saving faith? Justify your answer in light of verses 18-24. Does
verse 24 indicate that Simon really repented? Were the apostles
too proud to preach to the small villages? (8:25).

From this passage of Acts, list spiritual lessons taught about:

> Christian Service
> Ministry
> Greatness
> Right Relation to God.

EXPLANATIONS

1) "They were all scattered . . . except the apostles" (8:1*b*).
As indicated earlier in this lesson, most of those scattered were
probably the Hellenist believers, reaping exile as their punishment
for being closely associated with their leader Stephen and sponsoring the teaching he propagated. The apostles were spared
banishment because they were Hebrews, and they wisely remained at Jerusalem to nurture the nucleus of believers for the
demands of the days to come.

2) "Philip" (8:5). This is not the apostle of 1:13, but one of the
seven deacons (6:5). He is known as Philip the Evangelist. As
successor to his colleague Stephen, he was the first of the leaders
of the church to break through the barriers of Jewish isolation.

3) "Prayed . . . that they might receive the Holy Spirit" (8:15).
God allowed a delay of the phenomena[2] in order to officially as-

---

[2]We do not know what the external manifestations were, but very likely
they were similar to those at Pentecost Day. Whatever they were, Simon
was captivated by them.

sociate the Samaritans' experience with the apostles of the church. The presence of Peter and John was a token of the first extension of the Christian fellowship to include non-Jews. Such a delay was not repeated again in Acts, for it was a special situation. It therefore should not be taken as a normative Christian experience.[3]

4) "Gall of bitterness" (8:23). Gall was an extremely bitter herb. Read Deuteronomy 29:18b. Compare also Hebrews 12:15. The gall offered Jesus on the cross (Matt. 27:34) was a bitter wine containing stupefying drugs.

5) "They started back" (9:25). Philip probably accompanied Peter and John.

FURTHER ADVANCED STUDY

1) The subject of unclean spirits, or demons, appears in this lesson. Study demonism in the New Testament days, and today. For outside reading consult: *Spiritism and the Fallen Angels*, James M. Gray; *Between Christ and Satan*, Kurt E. Koch; *Demon Possession and Allied Themes*, John L. Nevius; *Biblical Demonology*, Merrill F. Unger. (An extensive bibliography of this subject appears at the end of Unger's volume.)

Articles in *The International Standard Bible Encyclopaedia*: "Divination" (pp. 860-63), "Magic, Magician" (pp. 1963-64), "Witch, Witchcraft" (pp. 3097-98), "Demon" (pp. 827-29).

2) Matthew 10:5 says: "These twelve Jesus sent out after instructing them, saying, 'Do not go in the way of the Gentiles, and do not enter any city of the Samaritans.'" Compare this with Jesus' words of Acts 1:8, and explain the change.

WORDS TO PONDER

"Not right before God" (8:21).

---

[3]See John F. Walvoord, *The Holy Spirit* (Grand Rapids: Zondervan Publishing House, 1958), pp. 153-54, for a brief discussion of this problem. Refer also to commentaries for help on this passage.

LESSON 12

AN ETHIOPIAN SAVED

8:26-40

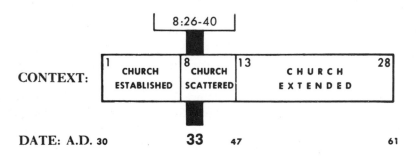

CONTEXT:

	8	13	28
CHURCH ESTABLISHED	CHURCH SCATTERED	CHURCH EXTENDED	

DATE: A.D. 30   **33**   47   61

PLACES: Road from Jerusalem to Gaza; Gaza-Azotus-Caesarea

INTRODUCTION

THE GEOGRAPHICAL PATTERN of evangelistic expansion in the first decades of the church followed *generally* the statement of Jesus in 1:8:

       1) Jerusalem
       2) Judea and Samaria
       3) remotest part of the earth

But this pattern was not so indelible as to exclude conversions of people of foreign nations in the early "Jerusalem" stage. The apostles saw this on Pentecost Day when many people from distant lands were saved. The story of this lesson cites another example of the gospel brought to a foreigner in the early days of the church. It was the Lord who used an angel and the Spirit to clearly direct His servant to the mission.

136

PREPARATION FOR STUDY

1) Refer to maps of Judea and North Africa and acquaint yourself with the following geography: Ethiopia; roads from Jerusalem to Gaza, and from Gaza to Caesarea via Azotus.

2) Read the passage from the Old Testament which the eunuch was reading aloud when Philip came upon him (Isa. 53:7-8). Compare the rendering of these two verses in various versions. Continue this comparative study by referring to the translations of Acts 8:32-33 in those same versions. When you have completed this study you will have learned some worthy suggestions on the intent of Isaiah 53:8. If you have not already done so in the present study, read all of Isaiah 53, keeping in mind that the eunuch had probably read much of Isaiah before he met Philip.

3) As you approach this passage of Acts, recall Philip's recent experience in Samaria, and what he has been doing since then (8:25). Try to visualize what Philip was thinking in regard to his next step. Whatever was going through his mind, he received clear instructions from the Lord for his next move (8:26).

ANALYSIS

1) The segment of this study may be divided into three paragraphs, as shown.

2) As you read the text, observe the detail Luke furnishes concerning the setting and action. Visualize the story as you read. Notice the contrast of atmosphere, as compared with the noisy and violent scenes of the first chapters of Acts.

3) Proceed with your analysis, recording your observations on the analytical chart. Complete the studies suggested below the accompanying chart.

4) This passage is one of the best biblical portions showing personal evangelism in action. From your observations of Philip's part in the eunuch's conversion, list the essential elements of personal evangelism.

5) In what ways was the Ethiopian official prepared for the gospel message?

Acts 8:26-40

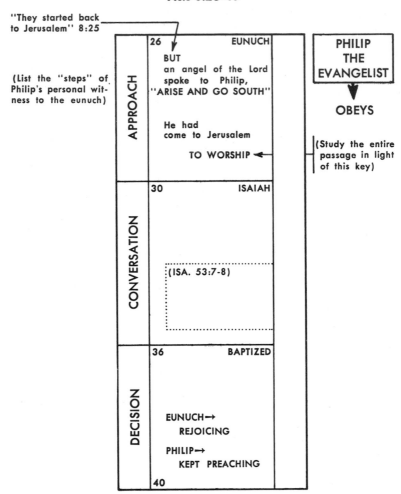

"They started back
to Jerusalem" 8:25

(List the "steps" of
Philip's personal wit-
ness to the eunuch)

APPROACH

26   EUNUCH

BUT
an angel of the Lord
spoke to Philip,
"ARISE AND GO SOUTH"

He had
come to Jerusalem

TO WORSHIP

CONVERSATION

30   ISAIAH

(ISA. 53:7-8)

DECISION

36   BAPTIZED

EUNUCH→
    REJOICING

PHILIP→
    KEPT PREACHING

40

PHILIP
THE
EVANGELIST

OBEYS

(Study the entire
passage in light
of this key)

1. Follow through a study of Philip the Evangelist, beginning with his obedience.
2. Notice contrasts in the passage. Compare the beginning and end.
3. How often does the word "Jesus" appear? Any references to God?
4. What is the relationship of "angel of the Lord" to "Spirit" in the first paragraph?
5. Make a study of the triad "understand . . . reading . . . guides" in light of the context.
6. Starting with the theme of "worship" (shown), indicate what each paragraph contributes to the subject.

6) What is the practical significance of the Ethiopian's invitation of verse 31; of his questions of verses 34 and 36?

7) What aspects of Jesus' life are brought out in the lines quoted from Isaiah?

8) Can one conclude from verse 36 that water baptism is a requirement for salvation? Has Luke recorded everything Philip said to the eunuch? (note 8:35).

9) What elements of the miraculous do you find in this passage?

10) What valuable lesson for Christian service is taught by 8:40?

EXPLANATIONS

1) "Gaza" (8:26). The old city of Gaza, located about two miles inland from the sea, was destroyed in 93 B.C., and rebuilt on the coast in 57 B.C. Thereafter the old site was known as Desert Gaza. As the NASB indicates, the word "desert" may either describe the city or the road to the city. Actually there were several routes from Jerusalem to Gaza. One went by way of Bethlehem and Hebron, and thence through a desert region. The direct route to Egypt turned south at the Old Gaza, since there was no need to go the extra two miles to the coastal city.

2) "The Spirit of the Lord snatched Philip away" (8:39). This was a miraculous event, the details of which are not given. (Why do the biblical records of miracles exclude details?) From Azotus to Caesarea, at least, Philip traveled in the usual manner.

3) "Azotus . . . all the cities . . . Caesarea" (8:40). Azotus, or Ashdod, was twenty miles north of Gaza, and Caesarea was fifty miles beyond Ashdod. Between Ashdod and Caesarea were located such Gentile cities as Jamnia, Lydda, Joppa and Antipatris. The prestige of Caesarea is seen in the fact that the official residence of the Roman procurator of Judea was located here. Of this Caesarea Rackham writes, "The name of Caesarea which concludes this section marks a great extension of the church."[1] It is of significance also to note that Philip apparently made his home here for the next twenty years, raising a family during that time. Luke does not bring him into the Acts story again until 21:8.

[1] Richard B. Rackham, *The Acts of the Apostles* (13th ed.; London: Methuen & Co. Ltd., 1947), p. 124.

FURTHER ADVANCED STUDY

1) Personal evangelism, or soul-winning, is as important as it is neglected in the ministry of the church today. Beginning with this classic passage, pursue your study of this subject further in Acts and in other New Testament books. Study especially how Jesus dealt with individuals about their souls.

For an outside reading project, here are some recommended books: *The Art of Soul Winning*, Murray W. Downey; *God-Centered Evangelism*, R. B. Kuiper; *Personal Evangelism*, J. C. Macaulay and Robert H. Belton; *The Secret of Soul-Winning*, Stephen Olford, *The Soul-Winner*, Charles Haddon Spurgeon; *How to Work for Christ*, R. A. Torrey; *Personal Soul-Winning*, William Evans.

2) The subject of water baptism is an intriguing one. In studying in this area, consider the following:

a) water baptism in pre-Christian days

b) the history of water baptism in post-apostolic days

c) etymology and usage of the Greek word *baptizo* in biblical and extrabiblical sources

d) various views of water baptism as to mode and time

e) purposes of water baptism and its relation to regeneration

For outside reading representing different viewpoints, consult the various articles by different authors under the title "Baptism," in *The International Standard Bible Encyclopaedia*, Volume I, pages 385-401.

WORDS TO PONDER

"Do you understand what you are reading?" (8:30).

LESSON 13

SAUL SAVED

9:1-19*a*

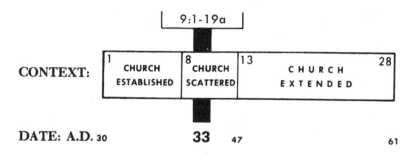

CONTEXT:

1 CHURCH ESTABLISHED	8 CHURCH SCATTERED	13 CHURCH EXTENDED 28

DATE: A.D. 30   **33** 47   61

PLACES: Road to Damascus; house of Judas on Straight Street in Damascus

INTRODUCTION

As THE PERSECUTION against the believers mounted, their dispersion to cities and villages multiplied in direct proportion. Luke has already cited the evangelistic witness to Samaria and the coastal region from Gaza to Caesarea. From the present chapter we learn that the disciples had settled down in another key city, Damascus.[1] Geographically, the thrust outward from Jerusalem was a solid one, as shown by the diagram on page 142.

It was when the persecution against the church had reached a peak through the fanatic labors of the arch-persecutor Saul, who was not even content to let the believers live in such distant cities as Damascus, that God came down and struck Saul to the

[1]There were some believers in Damascus before the persecuted saints arrived from Jerusalem, but their number was perhaps small (Ananias was one of them).

141

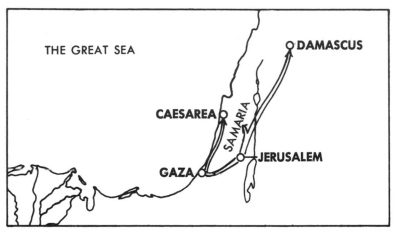

ground. In Blaiklock's words, "the rabid persecutor was a tormented man, soon to be brought to surrender, and destined to be the greatest name in the history of the Church."[2] The wonderful miraculous conversion of a man who called himself the chief of sinners is the subject of the present lesson.

PREPARATION FOR STUDY

This is the appropriate time to become acquainted with the early life of Paul.[3] The sovereign ways of God in foreordination are remarkably demonstrated in Paul's three-phased life, shown in relation to Christ and the early church. See accompanying chart.

You will find it very helpful to consult a book describing Paul's early life. (James Stalker's *Life of St. Paul* is excellent, written in popular style.) Space does not permit more than this tabulation:

[2]E. M. Blaiklock, *The Acts of the Apostles* (Grand Rapids: Wm. B. Eerdmans Publishing Co., 1959), p. 79.

[3]The main sources of information concerning Paul's early life are the brief references made here and there in Acts and in his epistles. Other aspects of his early life may be inferred with a fair degree of probability from other considerations. Volumes devoted to the life of Paul demonstrate how much of Paul's early life may be constructed with such a minimum of sources. Note: Saul is called Paul (a Roman name) for the first time in Acts 13:9. After that, Luke always refers to him as Paul. (Paul uses "Saul" in describing his conversion experience in 22:7, 13; 26:14.) The significance of the two names will be discussed later in the manual under 13:9.

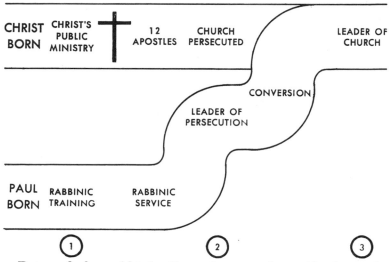

Date and place of birth: About the time of Jesus' birth,[4] in the city of Tarsus.

Home: Father—a strict Pharisee, native of Palestine, a Roman citizen, merchant by trade. Mother—probably a devout woman. Paul had at least one sister.

Education: Learned trade of tent making. May have matriculated at University of Tarsus. Rabbinical training at Jerusalem, under Gamaliel.

Post-school years: Probably served in synagogues outside of Palestine, returning to Jerusalem some time after Christ's ascension.

*   *   *

Refer to the map on page 131 to acquaint yourself with the general route of Saul's journey to Damascus. As you are reading the passage of this lesson, maintain a mental picture of who Paul really was, what his life had been, and what was the zeal of his heart. Recall also that the memory of being a consenting witness to the stoning of Stephen kept haunting him as a prick of inner guilt (cf. 22:20).

---

[4]This is a strong likelihood when one considers that in A.D. 33 (Stephen's death) Paul was a "young man" (Acts 7:58), and in A.D. 61 he calls himself an aged man (Philemon 9).

ANALYSIS

1) Divide this passage, Acts 9:1-19*a*, into the three paragraphs shown. Read through the text at least twice, underlining phrases about which you will want to make a special note in your textual re-creation and subsequent studies.

2) Proceed with your textual re-creation, observing and recording related studies on your analytical chart. You will notice that Ananias is an important character in the passage. Record the main characters from each paragraph in one of the narrow vertical columns.

3) There are many bold contrasts in this passage. Among them, observe these: (1) Saul: beginning and end of the segment; (2) contents of beginning and end of first paragraph; (3) reactions to Jesus by Paul and Ananias.

4) Complete the studies outlined below the accompanying chart.

5) At what time during this narrative do you think Saul was saved? Do you think Saul had previously considered the possibility that he might be wrong about who Jesus really was?

6) Was Jesus' question "Why are you persecuting Me?" answered?

7) Why do you suppose God caused so many external phenomena to attend Saul's spiritual experience? What were the lessons for Saul? What were the various spiritual experiences of Saul during this time?

8) What spiritual lessons do you learn from this story of Ananias?

9) Name three or four truths that are prominent in this passage.

EXPLANATIONS

1) "Damascus" (9:2). Damascus was an ancient city, an important junction enroute from Palestine to Assyria and Babylon. The gospel had been introduced here even before the persecuted Christians arrived from Jerusalem. The city had many synagogues, serving between ten and twenty thousand Jews. This large number of Jews accounts for Saul's personal concern over the threat of the gospel.

A MAN FROM TARSUS
Acts 9:1-19a

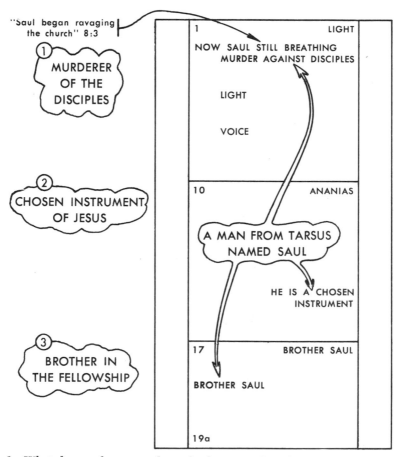

1. What does each paragraph teach about Jesus? (Third paragraph only implies some truth about Jesus.)
2. Notice the various ways the believers are referred to throughout the segment.
3. Notice the various ways Saul is referred to in the last two paragraphs.
4. Study the conversation between Ananias and Jesus. Notice Ananias' use of the word "Lord." How does the usage differ?
5. What is the status of Saul during the time period of each paragraph? Record this in one of the vertical columns.
6. In view of the context of the segment, what is the significance of the statement, "I will show him how much he must suffer for My name's sake" (9:16)?

2) "Belonging to the Way" (9:2). This was one of the earliest designations for the believers (see also 19:9; 22:4; 24:14, 22). It referred to the believers' way of life, and also to the way of salvation which they preached (cf. 16:17; 18:25).

3) "A voice saying" (9:4). Jesus spoke the words in Aramaic, the vernacular of Palestine. (Paul referred to Aramaic as the "Hebrew dialect" 26:14.) What was the spirit in which Jesus spoke the words, "Saul, Saul, why are you persecuting Me?" Why do you suppose Jesus repeated the name Saul? Compare "Martha, Martha" (Luke 10:41); "Jerusalem, Jerusalem" (Luke 13:34); "Simon, Simon" (Luke 22:31).

4) "Ananias" (9:10). Ananias is further described in 22:12. Beyond this, nothing more is known of him. He apparently was not one of the persecuted believers from Jerusalem. Ananias was the first Christian brother to welcome Saul into the fellowship.

5) "Saints" (9:13). This is the first of four such references to the believers in Acts (others: 9:32, 41; 26:10). It came into common usage shortly after, as seen by its frequent occurrence in the epistles. The word has a double connotation of "holiness" and "separation."

FURTHER ADVANCED STUDY

1) What is involved in the experience of soul conversion as seen from Paul's conversion? Arrive at conclusions that apply universally. For outside reading on one aspect of conversion, consult Robert O. Ferm's *The Psychology of Christian Conversion.*

2) "How much he must suffer for My name's sake" (9:16). Study the subject of "Suffering of the Saints" as the New Testament sheds light on this vital theme. A concordance will direct you to many biblical references. For related outside reading consult: *The Suffering Saviour*, F. W. Krummacher; *The Problem of Pain*, C. S. Lewis; *Sharing His Suffering*, Peter H. Eldersveld; *In the Arena of Faith*, Erich Sauer; *Christ in His Suffering*, Klaas Schilder.

3) Study the word "saints" in the New Testament and combine this with a study of the common words "holy," "sanctify" and "sanctification." Recommended outside reading: *Faith and Sanc-*

tification, G. C. Berkouwer; *The Fullness of Christ*, D. Stuart Briscoe; *He That Is Spiritual*, Lewis Sperry Chafer; *Holiness— The False and the True*, H. A. Ironside; *Born Crucified*, L. E. Maxwell; *The Normal Christian Life*, Watchman Nee; *Life on the Highest Plane*, Ruth Paxson; *Holiness*, J. C. Ryle.

WORDS TO PONDER

"He is a chosen instrument of Mine" (9:15).

SAUL'S FIRST MINISTRIES

9:19*b*-31

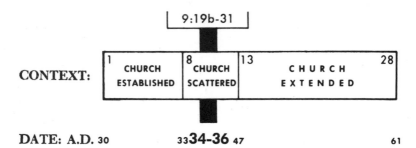

CONTEXT:

9:19b-31

1 CHURCH ESTABLISHED	8 CHURCH SCATTERED	13 CHURCH EXTENDED 28

DATE: A.D. 30   33**34-36** 47   61

PLACES: Damascus; Jerusalem; Caesarea

RULERS: Aretas, king of Arabia (9 B.C.—A.D. 40)
　　　　An ethnarch of Damascus
　　　　Marcellus, governor of Judea (A.D. 36-38)
　　　　Jonathan, high priest (A.D. 36-37)

INTRODUCTION

THE BIG TEST that comes to a leader or person of influence in society or government on his conversion to Christ is the test of the next day when he faces the crowd again and lets his new colors be known. The temptation to seal one's lips, retreat to a hidden corner or merely take a neutral stand on issues is not small. Perhaps the zeal which spurred Saul in his persecuting activities transferred to his new life as a believer so that courage and boldness were not mountains for him to climb. But what about *pride?* Saul had been the man of the hour, the champion of the cause of Judaism in the face of the foe of the "fanatic"

148

believers. Whatever turmoil existed within his soul regarding this, he won the contest—surely with the Spirit's help—and immediately began to proclaim Jesus. It was an astounding reversal, explainable only by the genuineness of his conversion.

There was another test at this time—a test of the church's reception of Saul into their fellowship. If Saul had been rejected by the church, he might have wandered about the streets as a virtual orphan. Some hesitated to take him in, even as today some Christians remain aloof from the new convert, imposing a man-made probation on him. It is a cruel, cold world into which newborn babes of Christ arrive, and happily a warm hearth of welcome is found among the faithful of God's people.

PREPARATION FOR STUDY

1) Before reading Luke's narrative of this lesson, place yourself in Paul's position. You have just gone through the experiences of 9:1-19a. What would be your next moves? Write down the various possible decisions and moves which Paul might have made, involving time, places, people, ministry. Having done this, you will appreciate all the more the story of 9:19b-31.

2) Barnabas appears in the narrative of this passage. Read 4:36-37 again, for Luke's earlier reference to him. Notice from 4:37 what the name Barnabas means.

3) Read Acts 22:17-21 as background for what transpires in 9:30 of the present study segment.

ANALYSIS

1) This is a comparatively short passage for analysis and may be divided into the three paragraphs as shown. This is a good opportunity to do extra work on your textual re-creation because of the shortness of the segment.

2) As you read the passage, keep in mind that this is the young convert Saul, who one day would be inspired of God to write such wonderful Christ-exalting lines as his Ephesian epistle. According to this passage of Acts, what was the core of Paul's gospel?

3) Proceed with your analysis, following the suggestions given with the chart on page 151.

4) As you conclude your study, gather together the practical lessons taught by the passage.

a) What is taught here about Christian fellowship?

b) What is taught about Christian growth?

c) God protects His children. Why was Saul hidden from his persecutors on these two occasions?

d) Does the basket experience suggest humiliation? Read Paul's later reflections on this in II Corinthians 11:29-33. You will find an interesting paraphrase of this passage in *Living Letters* by Kenneth Taylor.

e) What is implied by the phrase "*his* disciples" (9:25)?

f) What was Barnabas' threefold recommendation of Saul to the disciples? Are there any spiritual lessons here?

g) Is there any significance in the phrase "and he was with them" (9:28)?

h) What signs of spiritual health appear in 9:31?

EXPLANATIONS

1) "He is the Son of God" (9:20). This is the only occurrence of such a title for Jesus in Acts. It was one of the ways by which the Messiah was designated. Read II Samuel 7:14; Psalm 2:7; Hebrews 1:5.

2) "When many days had elapsed" (9:23). Somewhere in the interval of Luke's account of 9:19-26 Saul spent two to three years[1] in Arabia (Gal. 1:16-18).[2] There is good reason to place the Arabian visit between verses 21 and 22. Another plausible view is that the verses 9:19-22 are pre-Arabian, attached to his conversion date by "immediately"[3] (9:20); and that the verses

[1]Paul speaks of going to Jerusalem "three years later" (Gal. 1:18). According to Jewish reckoning this period of time could be from two to three years.

[2]Luke's omission of events in Saul's life does not jeopardize the accuracy of the record. Selectivity of the writer, which includes omission as well as inclusion, always supports the theme being developed by the writer. Other historical facts not mentioned in Acts include references to Paul's epistles written on the missionary journeys; some of the physical persecutions he experienced (cf. II Cor. 11); and many phases of his missionary tours (cf. 20:2).

[3]The "immediately" of Galatians 1:16 would not contradict this view. Luke uses the word sparingly; Paul uses it freely in Galatians to prove his argument. See Frank J. Goodwin, *A Harmony of the Life of St. Paul* (3rd ed.; New York: American Tract Society, n. d.), pp. 202-3 for a further discussion of this.

Acts 9:19b-31

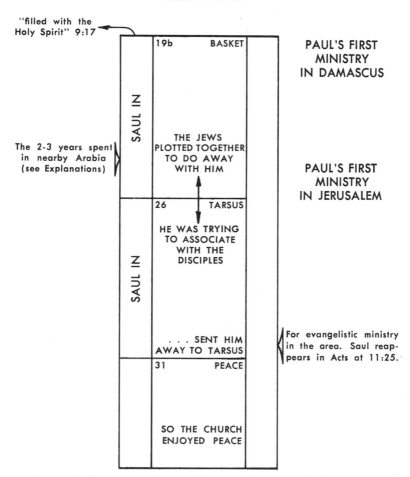

"filled with the Holy Spirit" 9:17

SAUL IN

The 2-3 years spent in nearby Arabia (see Explanations)

SAUL IN

19b   BASKET

THE JEWS PLOTTED TOGETHER TO DO AWAY WITH HIM

26   TARSUS

HE WAS TRYING TO ASSOCIATE WITH THE DISCIPLES

. . . SENT HIM AWAY TO TARSUS

31   PEACE

SO THE CHURCH ENJOYED PEACE

PAUL'S FIRST MINISTRY IN DAMASCUS

PAUL'S FIRST MINISTRY IN JERUSALEM

For evangelistic ministry in the area. Saul reappears in Acts at 11:25.

1. How is the last paragraph a conclusion to the section 8:1b–9:31 as well as to the present segment 9:19b-31?
2. How do the first two paragraphs differ from each other? Where is Saul in each paragraph? (Record in left-hand narrow column.) Who is Saul's contact in each paragraph? (Record in right-hand column.)
3. List the various things mentioned concerning Saul's first Christian ministry.
4. Compare the ending of the first paragraph with that of the second.
5. Observe the progression of the church's acceptance of Saul in the second paragraph.
6. Observe the various references to geography in the segment.
7. What is the grammatical core of verse 31?

9:23-25 are post-Arabian, since the Jews' plot brings on his escape to Jerusalem.

3) "Watching the gates" (9:24). Paul expands on this in II Corinthians 11:32-33.

4) "But Barnabas" (9:27). Barnabas already has appeared in Acts (4:36-37) before Saul's conversion, but only in reference to the church. Very likely he was acquainted with Saul before this time. Barnabas plays an important role in the remainder of Acts.

5) "The apostles" (9:27). According to Galatians 1:18-19, Peter (Cephas) and James (the Lord's brother) were the only two apostles[4] with whom Paul became intimately acquainted at this time. (The word "see" of Gal. 9:19 has the connotation of such an acquaintance, as compared with the milder word ."consult" of Gal. 1:16.)

6) "So the church" (9:31). Although Paul refers to the dispersed congregations as "churches" (cf. Gal. 1:22), Luke intentionally uses the singular here to emphasize the spiritual unity despite the geographical diversity (Judea . . . Galilee . . . Samaria). The inclusion of Galilee in this summary statement is also interesting in view of the fact that Luke has not chosen thus far to record any event involved in the church's expansion to that native land of Jesus.

FURTHER ADVANCED STUDY

1) The phrase "son of God" is so common in Christian terminology that it is in danger of losing its awesome implications. Study the New Testament usage of the expression and determine how it identifies Jesus.

2) It is open to conjecture as to what really was the activity of Saul in Arabia for the three-year period. What are the various possibilities? How do you think he spent this long time?

WORDS TO PONDER

"So the church . . . enjoyed peace, being built up" (9:31).

---

[4]James was considered one of the apostolic circle.

LESSON 15

PETER'S OUTLOOK CHANGED THROUGH A VISION

9:32—11:18

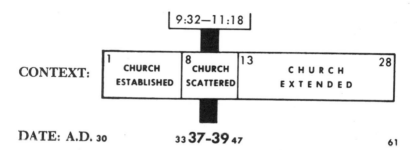

CONTEXT:

| 1 CHURCH ESTABLISHED | 8 CHURCH SCATTERED | 13 CHURCH EXTENDED | 28 |

DATE: A.D. 30   33 37-39 47   61

PLACES: Lydda, Joppa, Caesarea, Jerusalem

RULERS: Caligula (Gaius), Roman emperor (A.D. 37-41)
Marullus, governor of Judea (A.D. 37-41)
Theophilus, high priest (A.D. 37-41)

INTRODUCTION

THE SCATTERING of the Jewish believers which began on the day of Stephen's death was the first break in the solidarity of Jewish exclusivism which God would eventually liquidate. It was inevitable that Spirit-filled disciples should touch human hearts with whom they came in contact, regardless of race or religion. This is illustrated in the unrestricted expansion of the church as recorded by Luke in the previous section (8:1b—9:31) and summarized so triumphantly in 9:31.

But God wanted the Jews to hear clearly and in unambiguous

153

words that the gospel was for the Gentiles as well; for this reason
He led His disciples into the experiences recorded in 9:32–12:25.
The entire section might be called "The Gentile Mission," or,
as this manual's outline entitles it, "The Church Embraces Gentiles."

At this point in your study a more detailed survey of 9:32–
12:25 will be profitable. On a sheet of paper list the following
references, which divide the entire section into units (some of
these units are paragraphs, some are segments):

9:32	10:1	10:9	10:17	10:34	11:1	11:19	12:1	12:24	12:25

Read through the entire section, and record the general contents of each unit on your paper. This will help you become acquainted with the flow of contents. Now look for groupings of
materials and expand on the original survey of Acts which you
made in the beginning of your study.

The accompanying survey outline should not be referred to until after you have completed your own. The purposes for including an outline here are (1) to justify the manual's assignment of
sections by lessons; (2) to identify the manual's nomenclature for
outline references; (3) to suggest further survey studies.

The key study of the accompanying chart is that of the signs—
ways God used to tell Peter and the church that the gospel was
for Gentiles as well as for Jews.

Also shown on the chart is the distribution of the text for lessons 15 through 17 of the manual. As you proceed with the lessons, you will observe that the analytical chart method is not
used for all the segments of study. You may choose to do some
analytical charts completely on your own.

PART I (9:32–10:16)

Read this section primarily to learn how God was speaking to
Peter (and others of the apostles) concerning the gospel's mission to the Gentiles. Use any method of recording your studies
of this passage.

THE CHURCH EMBRACES GENTILES
Acts 9:32—12:25

9:32	10:1	10:9	10:17	10:34	11:1	11:19	12:1		12:24	12:25
Aeneas-Dorcas	Cornelius' Vision	Peter's Vision	Cornelius & Peter meet	Peter's Speech — Results	Peter's Report to Jerusalem	Antioch Mission — Barnabas-Saul	Herod vs. James & Peter	Conclusion	"the word . . . continued to grow"	12:25
Sign of Miracles	Sign of Visions		Sign of Conversions				Sign of Deliverance			
				CAESAREA		ANTIOCH				
GENTILE MISSION										
Lesson 15					Lesson 16		Lesson 17			

A. The Sign of Miracles (9:32-43). Some notes and questions for your study:

1. Lydda and Joppa were located in the general area of Gentile cities[1] where Philip had recently come to minister.
2. Who were the "saints" of 9:32?
3. How much of this coastal ministry of Philip is recorded by Luke?
4. What would the miracles of these paragraphs do for Peter and the church?
5. Note that Peter lodged in the house of a tanner (9:43). What does this suggest, in view of the fact that the tanner's occupation, involving the hides of animals considered unclean by Jews, was strictly frowned upon by Jews?

B. The Sign of Visions (10:1-16). Keep in mind that Cornelius the centurion was a Gentile, and an influential one at that. Read the two visions carefully, and answer the following questions:

[1]These cities, though populated by many Gentiles because of their location on the maritime plain, housed many Jews as well.

1. What clear evidence is there that the message in both visions was from God?
2. What was Cornelius told? In view of this, how would he respect Peter?
3. What was Peter told? In view of this, how would he respect Cornelius?
4. What was Peter's motive in first refusing the Lord's command? (10:14). The sheet probably contained clean as well as unclean animals ("all kinds," 10:12). Why would Peter have refused to eat even of the clean animals? How does this represent the Jewish exclusiveness which was the apostles' sin then? In view of the problem, what are the implications of the reply, "What God has cleansed, no longer consider unholy" (10:15)?

PART II (10:17-48)

While Peter was reflecting on his vision, the men whom Cornelius had dispatched in obedience to his vision appeared at the gate of the house where Peter was staying (10:17). Peter's vision had revealed nothing of Cornelius nor of the messengers. Now the Spirit, in what might be called a second vision, told Peter to accompany the messengers, for He said, "I have sent them Myself" (10:20).

Peter listened to their communication. While very general in scope, it initiated a relationship between the Jewish apostle and the Gentile centurion which would symbolize the universality of the gospel for the church. That communication was: "Cornelius . . . was divinely directed . . . to . . . hear a message from you" (10:22).

Peter knew only one message, the one he had been proclaiming ever since Pentecost. So it must have been at this moment that he began to relate the gospel to the heart of a Gentile and to understand God's intent in the vision of the great sheet.

Undoubtedly the leading apostle's experience at the prominent Gentile city of Caesarea was the key event of the church's first official acceptance[2] of its Gentile mission.

---

[2]The problem was to reappear later (Acts 15), when this test case concerning Peter and Cornelius would be cited.

PART III (11:1-18)

It was not enough for Peter and his six[3] Jewish companions to be convinced that Gentiles could be saved like the Jews without having had any prior covenant relationship to God, as symbolized by circumcision. The church as a whole, represented by those scattered throughout the regions, and those still living in the church "headquarters" city of Jerusalem, needed also to be convinced. So Luke's narrative of 11:1-18 satisfies our curiosity as to the sequel of chapter 10.

Read the eighteen verses carefully, noticing how orderly and convincingly Peter answered those who opposed his view. Your observations will supply answers to these questions:

1) What are the different references to the experience of the Gentile?

2) Notice the time reference of verse 15, and its significance (cf. 10:44).

3) What do you learn about Spirit baptism from Peter's application of Jesus' words? (v. 16).

4) How does 17b remind you of Gamaliel's words?

The problem of Jewish particularism unhappily was not settled once and for all at this time. This is probably because the Jerusalem church, while allowing for exceptions as in the case of Cornelius, assumed that Gentiles would still be required to come into their fold via Jewry, so that later, when they saw that Paul on his first missionary journey had thrown open the door to all Gentiles without such stipulations, the issue came to a head at the Jerusalem council (Acts 15). At any rate, as Bruce has written, "Jerusalem had at least admitted the principle of evangelizing Gentiles, and done so in time for a new advance farther north, as a result of which Gentiles were evangelized and converted to the Christian way on a scale which no one in Jerusalem had dreamed of."[4]

5) What are the three notes of acceptance cited in verse 18?

[3]Cf. 11:12b.
[4]F. F. Bruce, *Commentary on the Book of Acts* (Grand Rapids: Wm. B. Eerdmans Publishing Co., 1954), p. 236.

EXPLANATIONS

1) Refer to the map on page 131 for an identification of such places as Lydda (32), Sharon (35) and Joppa (36).

2) "Tabitha . . . Dorcas" (9:36). Tabitha was her Aramaic name; Dorcas, her Greek name.

3) "Cornelius a centurion . . . Italian Cohort" (10:1). The name Cornelius was a very common Roman name at this time. Originally a centurion commanded one hundred men, though this number varied later. A Roman legion consisted of ten cohorts, or bands. The commander of a cohort was called a chiliarch, or chief captain (cf. John 18:12). A cohort comprised six companies, each commanded by a centurion. Cornelius was commander of one company, or even possibly of an entire cohort.

4) "Unholy and unclean" (10:14). The ceremonial laws concerning unclean animals are prescribed in Leviticus 11.

5) "Worshiped him" (10:25). See NASB margin. Note: Don't overlook in any of your studies the many valuable marginal notes and references of the NASB.

6) "Unlawful . . . to associate with a foreigner" (10:28). Association as such with the Gentiles was not forbidden by the Mosaic law, but because Gentiles did not live by the ceremonial laws of cleanness, and since God commanded Israel not to defile themselves with unclean things, the Jews avoided all such intercourse with the Gentile world.

7) "Four days ago" (10:30). The reckoning of four days included the day of the utterance.

FURTHER ADVANCED STUDY

"God is not one to show partiality" (10:34). What does this passage teach about the equality of man? You may want to extend the scope of your study to other biblical passages.

Another suggested study related to the above subject concerns the fellowship of Christian groups and denominations. What should be the basis for such fellowship? How do differences of administration, organization and method relate to this subject?

WORDS TO PONDER

"While Peter was still speaking . . . the Holy Spirit fell" (10:44).

LESSON 16

MISSION-MINDED CHURCH AT ANTIOCH

11:19-30

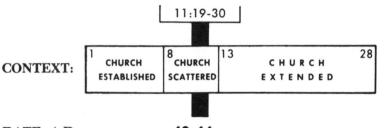

| 11:19-30 | |

CONTEXT:

1 CHURCH ESTABLISHED	8 CHURCH SCATTERED	13 CHURCH EXTENDED 28

DATE: A.D. 30   33 **40-44** 47   61

PLACES: Antioch, Tarsus

RULERS: Claudius, Roman emperor (A.D. 41-54)
Herod Agrippa I, king of Judea[1] (A.D. 41-44)
Simon, Matthias, Elionaeus, Joseph, high priests
(A.D. 41-47)

INTRODUCTION

THE MINISTRY of evangelistic witness—heralding the glad tidings of salvation—whether accomplished individually or en masse can never die as long as there are expendable Christians consecrated to God. We already have seen how persecution and many internal problems failed to kill the onward thrust of the gospel. With

---

[1]As a Roman province Judea was under the rule of procurators during all of the Acts period with the exception of this one period (A.D. 41-44), when it was made a part of the kingdom of King Herod Agrippa I, who already was ruling over the lands formerly under Herod Antipas (Luke 3:19; 13:32; 23:6) and Philip (Luke 3:1). See chart at the end of this manual.

the work continuing to spread to distant cities, would diversification (e.g., in personnel, methods, situations) tend to threaten the solidarity which the apostolic nucleus at Jerusalem enjoyed in the days immediately following Pentecost? One outstanding truth taught by Acts is that the solid expansion of Christianity in its early days is attributable to no less than the power of God channeled through the lives of weak human servants. Through the ragings of the wildest storms the church has managed to advance with miraculously low casualties, and today such things as a humble chapel in the Rocky Mountains and a Christian radio station in Ecuador bear testimony to the favor of God in granting His church continued growth and health.

By this time in your study of Acts you have probably observed that Luke has not given a consecutive narrative of the footsteps of any one person. He does this from chapter 13 to the end of the book, in relating Paul's ministry, but before chapter 13 the pattern is that of interchange—leaving an apostle in a certain city and recalling him into the narrative at a later point. This pattern is shown by the accompanying diagram.

The story of the present lesson is a bright one which reflects the spirit and tone of 10:44-48 and 11:18 by recording further victories of the apostolic band, including many Gentile conversions, some of which were as far north as Antioch. The story of verses 22-30 is a happy sequel to the Jerusalem church's conclusion of 11:18, but Luke also records in verses 19-21 the courageous and pioneering witness of the gospel to Greeks given about seven years previously by men of Cyprus and Cyrene who had left Jerusalem on Stephen's death and had traveled as far as Antioch. So while the majority of the disciples were only slowly and gradually learning of the universal intent of the gospel, a discerning few in remote places already were sharing their joy with others, without man-imposed conditions. It was appropriate therefore that the church at Antioch should sponsor Paul the missionary and become the mother church of the Gentile mission in Asia and Europe.

Luke's inclusion of this story in Acts is important from another standpoint. He had not referred to Saul since telling about the

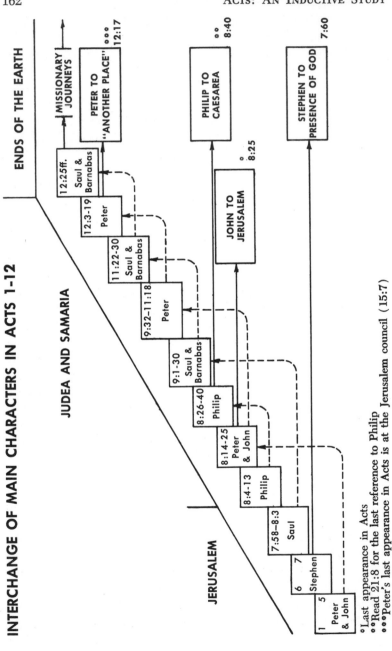

INTERCHANGE OF MAIN CHARACTERS IN ACTS 1-12

ENDS OF THE EARTH

MISSIONARY JOURNEYS

PETER TO "ANOTHER PLACE" ***
12:17

PHILIP TO CAESAREA **
8:40

STEPHEN TO PRESENCE OF GOD
7:60

JUDEA AND SAMARIA

12:25ff. Saul & Barnabas

12:3-19 Peter

11:22-30 Saul & Barnabas

9:32-11:18 Peter

JOHN TO JERUSALEM °
8:25

9:1-30 Saul & Barnabas

8:26-40 Philip

8:14-25 Peter & John

8:4-13 Philip

7:58—8:3 Saul

6 7 Stephen

JERUSALEM

1 5 Peter & John

° Last appearance in Acts
** Read 21:8 for the last reference to Philip
*** Peter's last appearance in Acts is at the Jerusalem council (15:7)

brethren sending him to Tarsus (9:30). In the near future Saul would begin a "worldwide" ministry of evangelization as the church's apostle to the Gentiles. Was there any opportunity for liaison between him and the leaders of the Jerusalem church in the interim, when the church could accept him more completely and even recognize him as one of their representatives and apostles? Paul's embassage to Jerusalem with Barnabas, as recorded in the passage of this lesson, was a convenient opportunity for the cementing of such relations.

Thus, this passage can be seen as a transitional section of Acts, with the evangelistic mission headquarters moving from Jerusalem to Antioch and with the leadership changing hands from Peter to Paul.

PREPARATION FOR STUDY

1) First, consult the map on page 131 to acquaint yourself with the geography of this lesson. (Cyrene, not on this map, is a port in North Africa. Cf. 2:10; 6:9; 13:1.) Phoenicia is the coastal region extending northward from Mt. Carmel for about 150 miles. Matthew referred to it as "the district of Tyre and Sidon" (Matt. 15:21). A journey by foot from Antioch to Samaria, such as the one taken by Paul and Barnabas (Acts 15:3), would traverse this Phoenician coast. The Antioch of this lesson is Antioch of Syria on the Orontes River. Cyprus is the large island about sixty miles due west from Antioch on Syria's coast. Barnabas was a native of this island. Refer to a Bible dictionary for a description of both Antioch and Cyprus. For this lesson also picture where Tarsus is in relation to Antioch, and try to visualize a foot-journey from the one city to the other.

2) Barnabas and Saul were last referred to in our study in Acts 9:27 and 9:30, respectively. Refer to your previous studies for the necessary review. Recall Barnabas' befriending attitude to the new convert Saul. Recall also why Saul was sent away to Tarsus.

ANALYSIS

1) For this segment (11:19-30) it is recommended that a new paragraph be made at verse 25, making three paragraphs in all.

2) As you read, keep in mind the content of 11:18. In this passage observe references to people, places and spiritual advance. Look for strong words and phrases here; there are many.

3) After you have read the passage three or four times, begin to record your study on the analytical chart. Follow the suggestions given below the accompanying chart.

4) What spiritual traits of Barnabas are obvious in this passage? Compare him with Stephen. In what ways was his task a delicate one?

5) Barnabas, the "son of encouragement," encouraged the Christians to remain true to the Lord. What is implied by Luke's recording this?

6) Notice the two parts of verse 21b: (1) "a large number who believed (2) turned to the Lord." Is the second clause redundant? How do you interpret this verse?

7) What was the Jerusalem church's interest in Antioch? Recall the earlier delegation of Peter and John to Samaria in connection with Philip's ministry.

8) What might have been Barnabas' reason for bringing Saul to Antioch?

9) Recalling why Saul had gone to Tarsus in the first place, how would Barnabas' seeking him out now be a blessing to Saul?

10) The Jerusalem church sent Barnabas to Antioch. The Antioch church sent Barnabas and Saul to the elders at Jerusalem. In what way was Saul's inclusion significant in light of his future evangelistic ministry?

11) List some of the major spiritual lessons taught by this passage.

EXPLANATIONS

1) "Antioch" (11:19). Antioch of Syria is located on the Orontes River, fifteen miles inland from the sea. When Syria was brought into the Roman Empire in 64 B.C., the city became a free city. During the days of Acts it was the third largest city of the empire, surpassed only by Rome and Alexandria. Although Antioch was a cosmopolitan city of various races and religions, it was predominantly a Gentile city. The city was branded with a wide

Acts 11:19-30

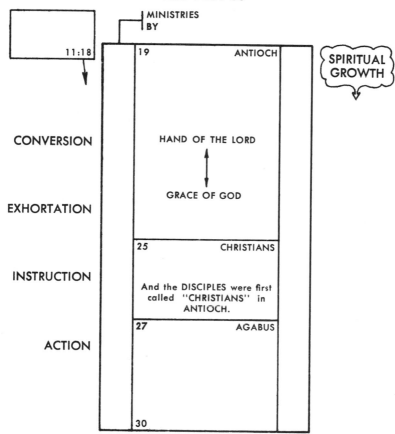

1. Compare 11:19-20 with 11:18.
2. The phrase "spiritual growth" aptly represents the story of this segment. Record such a study in the column shown. In the left-hand narrow column, identify the ministers of the gospel.
3. The duration of the action of the second paragraph is given; estimate the time element of the other paragraphs.
4. Study the ministry of the Word here.
5. What is implied by such a title as "Christian" being applied to a believer? What other spiritual traits appear in this passage? Don't overlook the third paragraph.
6. Compare the phrases "hand of the Lord" and "grace of God."
7. In the first paragraph, the Jerusalem church sends Barnabas to help the Antioch church. Compare this with the closing of the passage.
8. Compare the ministry of encouraging (11:23) with that of teaching (11:26).

reputation of loose morals. It is very possible that Luke was a native of Antioch.

2) "The disciples were first called Christians in Antioch" (11:26). It was probably the Gentiles who applied the word "Christians," for the Jews would avoid identifying the "apostates" with their Messiah—which the title "Christ" connotes.[2] Until this time the disciples referred to each other by such names as believers, disciples, saints, brethren, and those of the Way. The word "Christian" became part of their vocabulary after this time (see I Peter 4:16).

3) "Prophets" (11:27). The gift of prophecy was one of the spiritual gifts given to the apostolic church, described by Paul in I Corinthians 12:28; 14:29ff; Ephesians 4:11. (Read also Acts 13:1; 15:32; 21:9-10; Eph. 2:20; 3:5; Rev. 22:9.) Whatever revelation was given came from the Holy Spirit. Agabus is referred to in Acts only here and at 21:10.

4) "To the elders" (11:30). This is the first appearance in Acts of a reference to this office in the Christian organization. We have already observed some of the functions of elders in their rule of the Jewish synagogues; it is possible that the Christians established the office of elder after the Jewish pattern. *The Wycliffe Bible Commentary* suggests that probably "the believers constituted a number of house congregations in several homes, and the elders may have been the leaders of these several congregations" (see Acts 15:6, 23).[3]

FURTHER ADVANCED STUDY

1) The chapters of Acts covered by the last few lessons reveal that the church was not more than fifteen years of age when it came to the place of rather extensive organization. Make a study of New Testament church polity, including such areas as the local church's membership, offices and discipline, and the relation of the local churches to a centralized authority. You also may want

[2]The Jews referred to the believers as Nazarenes (cf. 24:5), in line with the then current proverb that nothing good could come out of Nazareth (John 1:46).
[3]Charles F. Pfeiffer and Everett F. Harrison (eds.), *The Wycliffe Bible Commentary* (Chicago: Moody Press, 1962), p. 1145.

to include in your study the major differences of church organization found between the various denominations today.

2) Considering the body of knowledge Barnabas and Saul had at the time, construct what you think was the curriculum of their one-year Bible instruction at Antioch.

WORDS TO PONDER

"But there were some . . . speaking to the Greeks also" (11:20).

GOD'S DELIVERANCE OF PETER FROM PRISON

12:1-25

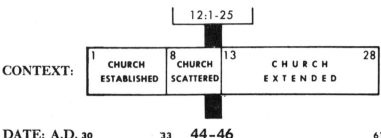

CONTEXT:

12:1-25		

1 CHURCH ESTABLISHED	8 CHURCH SCATTERED	13 CHURCH EXTENDED 28

DATE: A.D. 30   33   **44-46**   61

PLACES: Jerusalem; Caesarea

RULERS: Emperor Claudius
King Herod Agrippa I

INTRODUCTION

BEFORE LUKE PROCEEDED to write of the "acts" of Paul (chapters 13–28), he recorded one last memorable experience of Peter as a conclusion to the "acts" of Peter.[1] Chapter 12 is also a fitting conclusion to the context section *The Church Embraces Gentiles* (9:32–12:25), for God's deliverance of Peter was a sign of God's favor on the new program of unrestricted evangelization which Peter persuaded the church to undertake. For review purposes, the outline of the *Gentile Mission* section of Acts is repeated here.

[1]As has already been indicated, Peter appears once more in Acts, at 15:7.

GENTILE MISSION

9:32	10:1	10:17	11:19	12:1	12:24-25
SIGN of MIRACLES	SIGN of VISIONS	SIGN of CONVERSIONS		SIGN of DELIVERANCE	CONCLUSION
		CAESAREA	ANTIOCH		

In studying this chapter, you may choose to construct an analytical chart completely on your own. If so, make your own paragraph divisions. The last verse should be omitted from the segment, for its real relation is to 11:30. A suggested set of paragraph divisions is at verses 1, 7, 12, 18, 20.

PREPARATION FOR STUDY

You should be acquainted with some of the following historical background facts which are related to this passage.

A. Names

1. HEROD. This Herod was Herod Agrippa I, grandson of Herod the Great. The procession of office is shown on the following page (dates given are terms of office):

Herod Agrippa I was a sincere patron of the Jewish faith, and for this he had cultivated the good will of the Jews. His opposition against the church at Jerusalem (12:1) at this time indicates that whereas the earlier persecution (arising over Stephen) was directed mainly against the Hellenist believers, the present opposition was aimed at the Jewish apostles themselves. The Jews of Jerusalem no doubt were incited over the fact of the church's new inclusive policy regarding Gentiles.

2. JAMES, brother of John (12:2). James was the son of Zebedee, older brother of John. Together with Peter, the three were a leading trio among Jesus' disciples. It may be recalled that

FIRST GENERATION	SECOND GENERATION	THIRD GENERATION	FOURTH GENERATION
	HEROD ANTIPAS Tetrarch[2] of Galilee, Perea 4 B.C.——A.D. 39		
KING HEROD THE GREAT Ruled over all Palestine 40-4 B.C. (Ruler at time of Christ's birth)	ARCHELAUS Ethnarch[3] of Judea,[4] Samaria, Idumea 4 B.C.——A.D. 6	KING HEROD AGRIPPA I Ruled over former domains of Antipas, Archelaus and Philip A.D. 37-41 King of Judea A.D. 41-44	KING HEROD AGRIPPA II Tetrarch of Chalcis and of northern territory A.D. 48-70
	HEROD PHILIP Tetrarch of Batania, Trachonitis, Auranitis 4 B.C.——A.D. 37		

Peter, James and John were the only disciples present at the raising of Jairus' daughter and Jesus' transfiguration, and they were the ones whom Jesus placed closest to Him during His Gethsemane praying (Matt. 26:37-39). Whatever was James' activity during the infant years of the church, it is not recorded in Acts. Prior to chapter 12 his name appears only in the list of the twelve apostles.

3. JAMES, half brother of Jesus (12:17). (Cf. Matt. 13:55; Mark 6:3; Acts 15:13; 21:18; I Cor. 15:7; Gal. 1:19; 2:9, 12; James 1:1.) James by this time had become one of the pillars of the Jerusalem church.

[2]The title "tetrarch" originally was used to designate a ruler over the fourth part of a kingdom or province. *The Westminster Dictionary of the Bible* says, "Eventually the word tetrarch was used loosely for a petty subject prince, even though the land was not divided among four such rulers. The Romans adopted the term and used it as a convenient title for a prince to whom they granted a small territory only, and whom they were unwilling to dignify with the authority and rank of a king. J. D. Davis and H. S. Gehman (eds.), (Philadelphia: The Westminster Press, 1944), p. 599. In some cases a tetrarch was called a king out of courtesy.

[3]An "ethnarch" was the governor of an ethnic group which usually administered its own laws, though it was subject to an alien people. As with the title "tetrarch," this title came to be applied with different connotations.

[4]When Archelaus was deposed in A.D. 6, Judea was placed as a Roman province under the rule of procurators until King Herod Agrippa I was made king of Judea in A.D. 41. On the king's death in A.D. 44, the rule of procurators was restored. (Refer to the historical chart above for other related dates.)

4. JOHN MARK. This is the first appearance of Mark in Acts (cf. 12:25; 13:5, 13; 15:37-39; Col. 4:10; Philemon 24; II Tim. 4:11). Mark was the cousin of Barnabas. It is generally believed that he became Peter's interpreter in Rome, and that his gospel was based on Peter's preaching. Mark probably was one of Luke's informants for parts of the story of Acts.

5. BLASTUS. Blastus was a high official of Herod's court. Steward of the treasury, he very possibly was won over to the people of Tyre and Sidon through bribery. The famine plaguing them at this time (cf. 12:20) may have been the one foretold by Agabus.

B. *Time*

Since the year of Herod's death was A.D. 44, the events of 12:1-23 are dated in that year.

C. *The Persecutions*

Herod's persecution against the church was the fifth persecution recorded by Luke. Do you recall the others? (Chapters 4, 5, 6, 8, 12.)

ANALYSIS

In making your own analysis of this passage, you will want to keep the paragraphs in mind as you work with the smaller details of words and phrases. The project on the next page suggests valuable lines of study to follow for the segment 12:1-24.

After you have thoroughly studied the chapter, consider the following applications:

1) What is taught about God's will? Why should James be allowed to be slain, and Peter spared? What would the church at Jerusalem have learned from this?

2) You have no doubt noticed the details of description which Luke furnishes in this chapter. What does this do to the narrative?

3) What is taught about prayer here? Is it possible that James was slain before the church was aware of Herod's program to ravage?

Acts 12:1-24

12:1	3	7	12	18	20	24
BRIEF OUTLINE:	P E T E R					
A STUDY OF HEROD						
THE WILL OF GOD						
POWER						

THE CLIMAX: 12:24

4) List truths taught here about:
   miracles
   human nature
   pride
   judgment

5) You have probably observed the contrast between verses 23 and 24. What vital truth may be learned from this? In connection with verse 24, recall 6:7 and 9:31.

6) Think back over the first twelve chapters of Acts and make a mental note of what were really the primary aspects of the church's ministry. Consider such things as the church's calling, message, power, problems, growth, purpose and prospects concerning the future. List things that come to mind.

FURTHER ADVANCED STUDY

1) Many lessons on prayer can be learned from this chapter. Make a topical study of prayer through the book of Acts. Include

in your study the need of prayer, intercession, sacrifice, perseverance, joy, unity of believers, answers to prayer.

2) Angels are part of Luke's narrative of Acts as well as of his
gospel. Study this subject of angelology as taught by these two
books.

WORDS TO PONDER

"The iron gate . . . opened for them by itself" (12:10).

LESSON 18

FIRST MISSIONARY JOURNEY

13:1–14:28

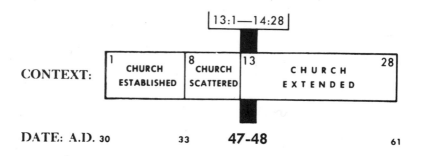

CONTEXT:

1 CHURCH ESTABLISHED	8 CHURCH SCATTERED	13 CHURCH EXTENDED 28

13:1—14:28

DATE: A.D. 30   33   **47-48**   61

PLACES: 1,500 mile journey (see map)

RULER: Sergius Paulus, proconsul of Cyprus

INTRODUCTION

CHAPTER 13 begins an entirely new section in Acts.[1] Antioch replaces Jerusalem as the base of operations or the mother-city of the church. Saul replaces Peter as the central figure of the evangelistic program. A mission field of all races and religions becomes the church's obligation, while the Jerusalem church continues to minister primarily to Jews. Home missions work in the homeland of Jerusalem, Judea and Samaria continues, but foreign missions work to Asia and Europe is added to the responsibility of the apostles.

[1]The last verse of chapter 12 might be considered as part of chapter 13.

174

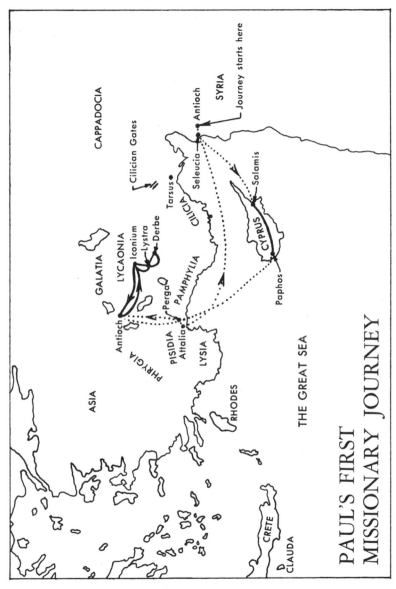

PAUL'S FIRST MISSIONARY JOURNEY

NOTE: In this and the two missionary journey maps to be shown later, the solid line represents the crusades of Paul's actual ministry while the dotted line represents the travel courses followed to the first cities of those crusades.

In the early chapters of Acts the church was continually confronted with new situations which demanded a pioneer spirit willing to adapt methods to the existing situation. With the overseas mission the demand for flexibility and novel strategies was even greater, since the patterns of the Israelitish worship were being pushed further into the background. Moreover, it was during Paul's missionary journeys that the apostle was inspired to write some of the holy epistles, and it is obvious from them that the interpretations and implications of the ABC's of the gospel message were becoming deeper and more advanced by revelation from God.

One might almost say that as of chapter 13 the church was leaving its teen-age years and entering into the first years of young adulthood. The challenge was big; the real rewards were spiritual and eternal. Only stalwart men of faith, filled with the Holy Spirit, could speed the gospel's cause. Concerning Paul's place in the picture, God had been in no hurry to prepare him for his worldwide ministry. Blaiklock writes: "The splendid deliberateness with which God forged His human tools is the great lesson of these [preparation] years . . . . At length, in God's good time, the door opened, and the events of half a life-time assumed final and complete significance."[2]

PREPARATION FOR STUDY[3]

1) If you choose to analyze any part or all of chapters 13 and 14 by the analytical chart method, the following divisions are recommended for identification of segments: 13:1-12; 13-41; 42-52; 14:1-20a; 20b-28. Of the five segments, the second and third should be given priority. You should have no difficulty identifying paragraph divisions within each segment. Remember that you do not necessarily follow the divisions of the version which you are studying.

2) Acquaint yourself with the geography of Paul's first missionary journey. If a topographical map is available, use it; it will

[2]E. M. Blaiklock, *The Acts of the Apostles* (Grand Rapids: Wm. B. Eerdmans Publishing Co., 1959), p. 90.

[3]If desired, the material of this lesson may be done as two lessons. The first section should then complete the work through PART I.

help you to appreciate the problems of travel in Paul's day and will also suggest at times the reasons for courses traversed. Observe especially the mountainous terrain of this area which Paul evangelized.

The most obvious geographical observation to be made from all of Paul's missionary journeys is that the direction of the advance was into the west. Paul was directed of the Spirit to follow the main current of history, commerce and civilization, ever keeping his eye on Rome, the heart of the world.

3) Try to think of the many things regarding the past, present and future that would be going through Paul's mind at this junction in his experience. Paul was a middle-aged man with fourteen years of preparation and some experience behind him for the Christian ministry (read Gal. 1:15–2:1). What great lesson had he probably learned by this time? What was the one passion of his soul?

ANALYSIS

PART I: THE COMMISSION OF BARNABAS AND SAUL (13:1-3)

These are just three verses, but they constitute a key passage in Acts, since the history of foreign missions begins here. Read the verses through a few times and begin to record observations.

1) Where was Saul's name placed in the list? (Note: The identity of the middle three names is unknown.) What was the five men's gift of ministering to the Lord at Antioch?

2) Who had called Barnabas and Saul to overseas work? Do you suppose they had been aware of this call before this time? What was the command to the other three?

3) What may be learned from the fact that the men were ministering (service at worship), fasting and praying during this time of commissioning?

4) What did laying on of hands symbolize? How intimate should the relationship be today between the missionary and the home church sponsoring him?

5) Observe the phrase "the work" in verse 2. Make it one of your major studies of this missionary journey to determine what that "work" really was.

6) Compare these opening verses of chapter 13 and the work they introduce with the opening two chapters of Acts and the work they introduce.

PART II: THE FIRST MISSIONARY JOURNEY (13:4–14:28)

First, read through the passage in one sitting. Visualize the action as Paul[4] and his companions move from place to place. Underline words and phrases in your Bible which you will want to study further as you return to their context.

Paul's first missionary journey may be thought of as comprising three missions:

Mission A (island): Cyprus, Barnabas' homeland, could be reached in a day's sailing and was a natural first stop on the evangelistic tour.

Mission B (inland): If Paul had already done evangelistic work in southeastern Cilicia by this time, we would expect him to want to move northwestward into the next districts and cities.

Mission C (return): This was a follow-up mission considered mandatory by Paul in view of the tense outward circumstances under which the converts had come to know the Lord as Saviour. On a sheet of paper record the outstanding facts of each mission as suggested by the accompanying outline.

In studying Paul's three missionary journeys, you should look primarily for three things: the *message* delivered, the *men* ministering and the *methods* used. Christian missions, the church's working arm, has one *message*—the gospel of the inspired Bible. Its *methods* are understandably diverse. Its *men* must be Spirit-filled apostles with a deep conviction of calling.

Refer to chapters 13 and 14 again and see how much the text reveals (explicitly or implicitly) concerning the following subjects:

[4]Notice the first use of the name Paul at 13:9. Recall also that up to this point the name of Barnabas has preceded that of Saul (e.g., 13:7), but from this point Paul takes the leadership (e.g., 13:13; 14:12; note the exceptions at 15:12, 25). Concerning Paul's names, Saul was his Hebrew name; Paul was his Roman cognomen. Of the latter Bruce writes: "The apostle, as a Roman citizen, must have had three names—*praenomen, nomen gentile* and *cognomen*—of which Paullus was his *cognomen.* . . . The apostle's *praenomen* and *nomen gentile,* unfortunately, have not been preserved." F. F. Bruce, *Commentary on the Book of Acts* (Grand Rapids: Wm. B. Eerdmans Publishing Co., 1954),n., pp. 264-65.

SUMMARY OF PAUL'S FIRST MISSIONARY JOURNEY

A.D. 47-48 (12 to 18 months)

13:1	13:4	13:13				14:21	14:26 14:28
COMMISSION	MISSION (A) Island	MISSION (B) Inland				MISSION (C) Return	HOMECOMING
	CYPRUS: ① SALAMIS ② PAPHOS		14:1 ① ANTIOCH OF PISIDIA	14:7 ② ICONIUM ③ LYSTRA	14:20 ④ DERBE	LYSTRA ICONIUM ANTIOCH PERGA ATTALIA	ANTIOCH OF SYRIA
	① Salamis Ministry: ② Paphos Ministry: Opposition: Miracle: Spiritual Fruit:	① Antioch Ministry: Opposition: Altered strategy: Spiritual Fruit: ② Iconium Ministry: Opposition: Spiritual Fruit: ③ Lystra Ministry: Miracle: Problem: Opposition: ④ Derbe Ministry: Spiritual Fruit:				RETURN VISITS Ministry: Spiritual Fruit:	MISSIONARY REPORT

The Message (Make a thorough analysis of Paul's sermon at Antioch, 13:16-41.)

1) to Jews
2) to Gentiles
3) to all

The Men

1) qualifications
2) commission
3) spiritual traits manifested

The Methods[5]

1) Work details:
    a) itinerary[6]
    b) staff duties
    c) varieties of ministry
    d) duration of ministry
2) Relationships
    a) within the staff
    b) to Jews; to Gentiles
    c) to secular and religious authorities
    d) to natural obstacles
3) Ministry concluded
    a) with follow-up program
    b) with indigenous church

After you have finished the above study, consider the following study suggestions:

1) Why does Luke so frequently refer to the Holy Spirit, as he does at 13:9, with reference to Paul?

2) What are some possible reasons for John Mark's leaving the evangelistic party at Perga? (13:13). Read Acts 15:36-39. Also,

[5]Your study into the next two missionary journeys will increasingly reveal more of the general policies followed by Paul.

[6]Occasionally in Acts or in Paul's epistles there are clues as to itinerary decisions. If Galatians was written to the churches at Antioch, Iconium, Lystra and Derbe, as seems likely, then Galatians 4:13-14 has something to say about part of Paul's itinerary on the first journey. For possible explanations, see Richard B. Rackham, *The Acts of the Apostles* (13th ed.; London: Methuen & Co., Ltd., 1947), pp. 204-205. It has already been suggested above why Cyprus was included in the first journey.

read Paul's later commendations of Mark (Col. 4:10; II Tim. 4:11).

3) Compare the three exhortations of Paul in his Antioch sermon recorded in 13:32, 38 and 40.

4) Analyze the complexity of the sequels to Paul's sermon (13:42-52). What truths are taught by this passage?

5) How do the verses 13:46-47 throw light on Paul's special ministry? Compare similar occasions of Paul's ministry at Corinth (18:6), Ephesus (19:9), and Rome (28:28). How does Romans 1:16, written by Paul at a later time, represent the apostle's position? Did Paul intend never to preach to a group of Jews again?

6) Explain the reason for the type of message Paul preached at Lystra (14:15-17). Compare this with Paul's other sermon of Acts delivered to a purely pagan audience at Athens (17:22ff).

7) What various ministries did Paul want to accomplish in his returning to Lystra, Iconium and Antioch? Notice by the map that Tarsus, Paul's hometown, was only 160 miles away from Derbe, by way of the Cilician Gates. What do you learn from this?

8) On the return trip the apostles preached the word at Perga, though no mention of such a ministry is cited on the forward part of the journey (13:13-14). Are there any explanations? Of course it must always be kept in mind that Luke's narrative is not intended to be exhaustive, and one cannot draw final conclusions from mere silence or omission. It is a characteristic of Luke, as of any historian, to select items to record that will serve his theme as a writer. Of this Blaiklock writes, "He is ruthless in his brevity when he narrates events without immediate significance in the plan of his story. He is prepared for repetition when he is setting forth important movements in the record."[7]

9) How do the verses 14:26-27 interpret what was meant by "the work" of 13:2?

EXPLANATIONS

1) "Helper" (13:5). The Greek word is translated as "attendant" in some versions. What John's duties were is not definitely known. They may have been any of the following: immediate follow-up of the apostles' work by instruction of the new

[7]Blaiklock, op. cit., p. 96.

converts; baptizing the believers; serving as an informant to Paul and Barnabas concerning the life of Jesus; ministering to the personal needs of Paul and Barnabas.

2) "Proconsul" (13:7). There were two types of Roman provinces: (1) those governed by procurators, responsible to the emperor; and (2) those governed by proconsuls, under the senate. Cyprus had been governed by a proconsul since 22 B.C.

3) "They went into the synagogue" (13:14). Rackham gives this description of the common layout of the synagogue interior: "The arrangements of the building were simple. At one end was the ark containing the books of the Law; a veil hung before it, and also lamps. At the same end were ranged, facing the people, the 'first seats' appropriated to the ruler and other dignities. In the centre was a raised platform, on which stood a lectern for reading and a seat for the preacher. The men and women were probably separated—how, exactly, we do not know."[8]

4) "Men of Israel, and you who fear God" (13:16b). The first phrase referred to Jews, the last, to Gentiles. Compare 13:26.

5) "Not . . . without witness" (14:17). Compare Romans 1:19-20.

6) "They spent a long time" (14:28). This was probably for about a year.

FURTHER ADVANCED STUDY

1) Read Paul's epistle to the Galatians, to get further insight into the spiritual traits of these saints whom he had led to the Lord, and also to understand more fully why Paul was so anxious to strengthen their faith by returning to their assemblies before traveling back to Syrian Antioch.

2) Do outside reading on the cities which Paul visited. One of the classics is W. M. Ramsay's *The Cities of Saint Paul* (N.Y.: George H. Doran Company, n.d.). Read also Jack Finegan's *Light from the Ancient Past* (Princeton: Princeton University Press, 1946), pages 252-96.

3) There has been difference of opinion over whether Galatians was written to the churches Paul evangelized on the first journey (South Galatian theory) or to the churches of Galatia

[8]Rackham, *op. cit.*, p. 207.

proper in the north, the area traversed on his second and third journeys (North Galatian theory). The former view, held by William Ramsay, has wider acceptance today.[9] J. B. Lightfoot has made a strong defense for the latter view.[10] Read Tenney, *New Testament Survey*, pages 264-68, for a clear presentation of the question, its implications and a solution.

WORDS TO PONDER

"He had opened a door" (14:27).

[9]A condensed version of Ramsay's view is given by Frank J. Goodwin, *A Harmony of the Life of St. Paul* (3rd ed.; New York: American Tract Society, n.d.), pp. 64-66.

[10]J. B. Lightfoot, *St. Paul's Epistle to the Galatians* (10th ed.; London: Macmillan & Co., 1890), pp. 18-35.

JERUSALEM COUNCIL

15:1-35

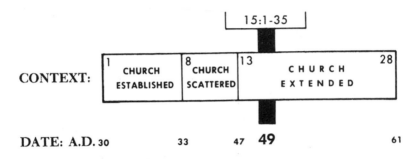

CONTEXT:

15:1-35

1 CHURCH ESTABLISHED	8 CHURCH SCATTERED	13 CHURCH EXTENDED 28

DATE: A.D. 30   33   47 **49**   61

PLACES: Syrian Antioch; Phoenicia and Samaria; Jerusalem

INTRODUCTION

LUKE'S ACCOUNT of the first years of the Jerusalem church makes it obvious that some of the brethren there were too proud to give up what they thought was an indissoluble ingredient of salvation —the works of the law of their father Moses. The constituency of this group of believers at Jerusalem at this time was mostly Hebrew Christians, the Hellenist believers having been scattered after Stephen's death. With the mass influx of Gentile converts into the fellowship of saints expanding to distant lands, many Jewish believers probably foresaw themselves soon being outnumbered by the "foreigners," not a pleasant prospect for them. After his experience with Cornelius, Peter had convinced most of the apostles and brethren that God had granted redemptive repentance to Gentiles as well as to Jews (11:18). But perhaps in the minds of these brethren a plus condition for salvation would

184

still hold for Gentiles in general, even though Cornelius himself did not submit to such rules as circumcision. When the report of the fruitful Gentile ministry of Paul and Barnabas in foreign cities reached Jerusalem, this was too much for some of those brethren. Without authority from the church (15:24), they went to Antioch to publicly refute the apostles' message.

PREPARATION FOR STUDY

1) First read 11:1-18 to recall Peter's earlier confrontation with the apostles and brethren at Jerusalem. Review also other ministries to Gentiles accomplished in chapters 8-12. Keep in mind that Paul's message on his first missionary journey was not a *different* message.

2) Read (1) of *EXPLANATIONS* section in this lesson for additional pertinent background.

3) Recall from your previous study in Acts the symbolic significance of circumcision. Why would circumcision be cited to represent other kinds of observances of Moses' law (note 15:5b)?

4) Read the passage in the Old Testament (Amos 9:11-12) which James quotes at 15:16-18. James usually quotes from the Greek Septuagint version,[1] which varies considerably here (especially Amos 9:12) from the Hebrew Massoretic text, the underlying text of our Old Testament versions.

Concerning Amos 9:12, either reading supports the main point James was making, as shown by the following: Massoretic Text: rebuilt tabernacle would possess all nations; Septuagint Text: all nations would seek the Lord.

Read also Paul's later exposition of this truth concerning Gentiles, found in Romans 15:8-12.

ANALYSIS

1) Because of the length of this segment your textual re-creation on the analytical chart must be abridged, especially in the third and fourth paragraphs. Divide the segment into five paragraphs of equal length on your chart, at divisions shown.

[1]The Greek Septuagint Old Testament was translated from the Hebrew Old Testament. The translation process from Hebrew to Greek was a natural cause for slight differences in phraseology. Other factors also account for the differences between the two texts.

2) After your first reading record your own paragraph titles in upper right-hand corners of paragraph boxes. Read through the passage one or two more times, noting key phrases as you read.

3) Notice groupings of paragraphs according to content. The middle three paragraphs record the deliberations of what is known now as the Jerusalem council.[2] Outline these three paragraphs in the left-hand narrow vertical column.

4) Proceed with your analysis study, recording observations and correlations on the analytical chart. Work also on the suggestions shown below the accompanying chart.

5) What notes of graciousness, tact, humility and perseverance are evident in this passage? How important are these in the Christian ministry?

6) Was any one man the key to the council's decision? Consider the implications of your answer.

7) How did the testimonies of Peter, Barnabas and Saul, and James complement each other in the advance of the argument?

8) Notice that the council's unanimous recommendation was a negative thing: abstinence. Compare this with the requirement sought by the legalists (15:1, 5). What was the intrinsic value of such abstinence? How did the letter attribute the recommendation to the Holy Spirit? (15:28).

9) Observe the various effects resulting from the council's letter. Account for such blessing of God.

10) Before leaving this passage spell out some of the truths taught here concerning:

> Way of salvation
> Christian living
> How to deal with divisions in the church.

EXPLANATIONS

1) It will be profitable at this point to weave other events into Luke's record. Paul refers to some of these in his epistle to the Galatians. There are various views on the exact order of chronology; the following order is the background for this manual's comments:

[2]The term "Jerusalem council" does not refer to the Sanhedrin of Jerusalem, but to a convention of leaders of the early church held in Jerusalem.

Acts 15:1-35

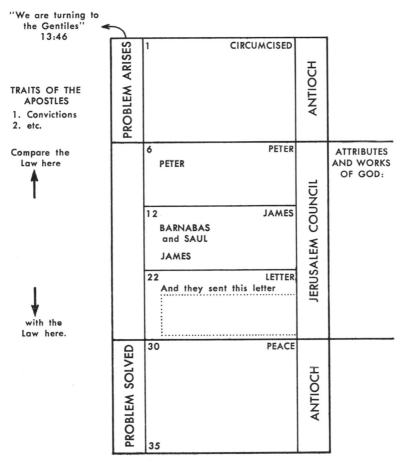

"We are turning to
the Gentiles"
13:46

TRAITS OF THE
APOSTLES
1. Convictions
2. etc.

Compare the
Law here

with the
Law here.

PROBLEM ARISES

1   CIRCUMCISED

ANTIOCH

6   PETER
PETER

12   JAMES
BARNABAS
and SAUL
JAMES

22   LETTER
And they sent this letter

JERUSALEM COUNCIL

ATTRIBUTES
AND WORKS
OF GOD:

PROBLEM SOLVED

30   PEACE

35

ANTIOCH

1. Complete the study of the traits of the apostles, shown throughout the segment.
2. Study the content of the speeches made at the council. Among other things, record attributes and works of God cited in connection with the subject being examined.
3. Note all references to the law in the passage. Look for the comparison suggested above on the chart.
4. James refers to Simeon, the prophets and Moses. What was his point in recognizing Moses? What were the principles recognized by the council in the abstinence concession?
5. Contrast the atmospheres of the first and last paragraphs.
6. Notice references to joy, and the reasons in each instance.

a) Soon after Paul's return from his first missionary journey to the South Galatian cities, he wrote *Galatians* to those young churches. The reason for the letter was that Judaizers had come to the young Christians and were luring them over to a legalistic concept of salvation. Read Galatians 1:6-7.

b) About the same time Peter arrived in Antioch from Jerusalem (Gal. 2:11ff). At first he mingled with the Gentile Christians, and also ate with them. But when certain Jewish brethren arrived from Jerusalem, he avoided the tables of the Gentiles and ate only according to the Jewish food laws. Even Barnabas joined him in the concession (Gal. 2:13). The motives of both Peter and Barnabas were obviously sincere.

c) Paul condemned Peter's action, because Paul wisely anticipated the inevitable outcome of such double standards by the church's leaders: instead of one church growing for the glory of God, two would emerge: a Jewish church and a Gentile church. Paul considered this to be totally inconsistent with the common grace and gospel of God. Obviously a synthesis of a *modus vivendi* (practical way of living) which would honor the Jewish heritage and promote the Gentile inclusion was needed.

d) Peter and Barnabas saw their mistake. But other Jews were not easily convinced, their position encouraged by certain men who had arrived from Jerusalem to continue the disturbance (15:1). The issue was vital enough to bring it to a showdown for official action by the church leaders at Jerusalem, and so the Antioch church sent an official party to Jerusalem for that reason (15:2).

2) "Abstain from" (15:20). The concession did not involve salvation; it was made in the interests of fellowship: (1) as a gesture of courtesy and respect to the Jews who had good reason to continue habits of purity and cleanliness in their living; and (2) to avoid laying any temptation to weaker brethren of Jewish birth. (Read Rom. 14:1ff. and I Cor. 8:1ff.) Also, to ask Gentiles to abstain from such things could serve advantageously in their

own living, making them more sensitive to the demands of holy living which their new life in Christ brought with its liberty.

3) "For Moses . . . has in every city" (15:21). Two plausible reasons are suggested as to why James spoke these words:

a) To alleviate the fears of the Pharisaic party in the Jerusalem church that with such a liberal policy the Gentile world would no longer learn the Holy Scriptures in a Jewish setting. James reminds them that the Word would continue to be taught in the synagogues which were located everywhere.[3]

b) To justify the recommendation of abstinence by noting that since Jewish brethren were dwelling in all parts of the world, the policy of respect should be universally applied.

FURTHER ADVANCED STUDY

1) Paul and other New Testament writers have much to say about Christian liberty and the evils of antinomianism. Make a thorough study of these important subjects in the New Testament. Relate the action of the Jerusalem council to your study.

2) With the help of outside historical sources, trace the history of the Jewish church in Palestine through the first two centuries. Look especially for the merging of the old into the new.

WORDS TO PONDER

"For it seemed good to the Holy Spirit and to us" (15:28).

---

[3]It was still difficult for many of the early Jewish believers to realize that true worship of God could take place outside the institution of Jewry.

SECOND MISSIONARY JOURNEY

15:36–18:22

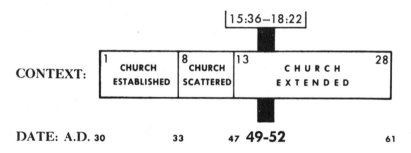

CONTEXT:	1 CHURCH ESTABLISHED	8 CHURCH SCATTERED	13 CHURCH EXTENDED 28

15:36–18:22

DATE: A.D. 30   33   47 **49-52**   61

PLACES: 3-4,000 mile journey (see map)

RULERS: Claudius, Roman Emperor
Gallio, proconsul of Achaia (A.D. 51-53)

INTRODUCTION

PAUL'S PASSION always was tuned to the need of the hour. With sanctified extrovert qualities he constantly was about the business of the gospel in the hearts of men, and cared not for riding any personal hobbyhorse. While the recent foreign mission was, from a human standpoint, uniquely his project, and the scars of his body and memories of the work were constant reminders of those memorable months, with discipline he had attached himself wholeheartedly to the next critical event of the hour, which was the Jerusalem council. Even when its work was over, he spent time preaching and teaching the Word at Antioch (15:35),

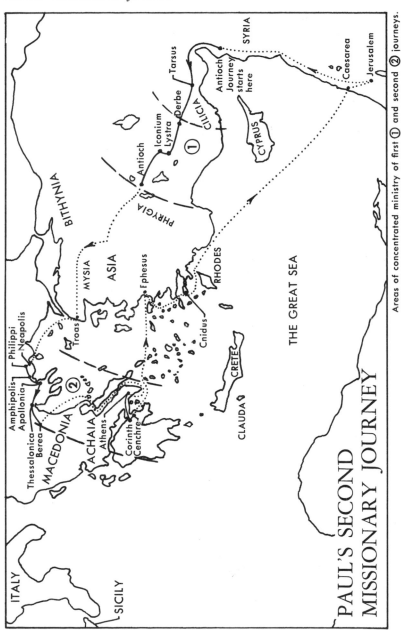

PAUL'S SECOND
MISSIONARY JOURNEY

Areas of concentrated ministry of first ① and second ② journeys.

very likely expounding on the very issue which the council had resolved. But now his job there was completed, so he could again fix his attention on the spiritual need of yonder lands. Talking with Barnabas, he said, "Let's visit the brethren again, and see how they are doing." Thus was born in the heart of Paul what has since been called the second missionary journey.

PREPARATION FOR STUDY

1) If you choose to analyze all of 15:36—18:22 segment by segment, the passage may be divided into the following five segments: 15:36—16:15; 16:16-40; 17:1-15; 17:16-34; 18:1-22. The last two segments are especially recommended for analysis.

2) Acquaint yourself with good topographical maps, such as those in the Westminster Historical Atlas,[1] of the lands of this second journey. Become acquainted with the names of the cities and areas visited before you read the text, just as you would study a road map in anticipation of a trip.

Read the descriptions given in a Bible dictionary of the following names of people and places:

People: Silas, Timothy, Jason, Epicurean and Stoic philosophers, Aquila and Priscilla, Claudius, Titius Justus, Crispus, Gallio and Sosthenes.

Places: Asia, Bithynia, Troas, Macedonia, Philippi, Thessalonica, Athens, Areopagus and Corinth.

3) Recall again that the missionary party did not have any of the modern modes of transportation and communication. This did not keep them from the long, arduous and sometimes dangerous journeys demanded by their goals.

SURVEY OF THE SECOND MISSIONARY JOURNEY

After reading the text once, draw the framework of the accompanying outline on paper. Then do your slower second reading, recording the highlights of the journey on the chart.

Note that this journey may be divided into three missions, as was true of the first journey. They are:

Mission A: Follow-up of the first journey

[1] George E. Wright and Floyd V. Filson (eds.), *The Westminster Historical Atlas to the Bible* (Philadelphia: The Westminster Press, 1946).

SECOND MISSIONARY JOURNEY
Acts 15:36—18:22

A.D. 49-52

15:36	15:41	16:6	16:11	17:1	17:10	17:15	18:1	18:18 / 18:22
Antioch	Syria Cilicia	Mysia Troas	Philippi	Thessalonica	Berea	Athens	Corinth	Ephesus Caesarea Antioch
	ASIA MINOR		**MACEDONIA**			**ACHAIA**		
PREPARATION & COMMISSION	MISSION (A)		MISSION (B)			MISSION (C)		RETURN
PERSONNEL								
DURATION								
ITINERARY DETERMINANTS								
MINISTRIES							I and II Thess. written from Corinth [2]	
KEY MESSAGES								
OPPOSITION & DELIVERANCE								
SIGNS & MIRACLES								
SPIRITUAL FRUIT								
KEY VERSES								

[2]It was in response to the report from Timothy concerning the Thessalonians (cf. Acts 18:5 and I Thess. 3:6) that Paul wrote the letters.

Mission B: Work in Macedonia (in response to the vision)

Mission C: Work in Achaia

From your study thus far, summarize those aspects of the journey which shed more light on the three large subjects of Message, Men and Methods, a study which you began in Lesson 18. This study will put due emphasis on those things which were vital in Paul's evangelistic crusade.

QUESTIONS ON THE JOURNEY'S OVERALL SIGNIFICANCE

1) When Paul left Antioch on this evangelistic crusade, he probably had certain objectives in mind in terms of geography. Looking at the map on page 191, what territories would have been the next logical goals?

2) As it turned out, what were the different determinants of itinerary along the way? Was Paul vacillating between conflicting directions or standards of enlightenment? What was the substratum principle underlying Paul's knowing the will of God as to the operation of the crusade?

3) Notice from the map at the beginning of this lesson that an important area surrounding the hub of Ephesus was practically ignored on this trip. What are the implications?

4) How much of Paul's ministry was to Jews? How much to Gentiles? After the events of the first journey, would you have expected more concentration on the latter?

5) In what ways were Paul's audiences ready-made in the various cities? How does this help to clarify his continuing ministry to Jews? Would an advance party, sent to each city to prepare the way for Paul, have helped his ministry?

6) On the basis of the record of both journeys, write out in a few sentences the major goal, message and method of Paul.

7) In what way was the ministry to Macedonia and Achaia a stepping stone in reaching Rome, Paul's ultimate goal?

8) Compare Paul's mission fields with those of the present day. Are all fields alike? Is fruit always evident? Is the mission's success measured by the exhilarating feelings of the missionary, or even by the popular reaction of the multitudes?

9) Luke does not describe the short deputation visit to Jerusalem (18:22) nor the longer stay at the supporting church of Antioch (18:23). Explain this intentional omission by Luke.

10) Toward the end of this journey Paul took the vow mentioned in 18:18. Assuming that at least the spirit of the vow resembled that of the Nazarite vow of Numbers 6:1-21, how relevant was such a spirit to all that Paul had experienced thus far from the hand of God in the evangelistic endeavor?

11) In what ways was Paul's second journey an extension of the missionary program begun on the first journey?

12) Show how the key verses which you have chosen and recorded for each section of this journey are related and how they summarize the mission which Paul accomplished.

QUESTIONS ON PAUL'S MINISTRIES AT ATHENS AND CORINTH

Athens (17:16-34)

1) What methods of witnessing did Paul use in Athens? How was he equipped for this?

2) What statements in the sermon itself were directed to the false doctrines of the Epicureans and Stoics?

3) What does the inscription "To An Unknown God" imply about the Athenians who worshiped at this altar? How did Paul interpret the inscription?

4) From Paul's argument of verse 29, of what substance is God shown to be?

5) In the context of verse 31, of what is the resurrection of Christ a proof?

6) What does this passage teach about: heathen idolatry, religiosity, adapting the gospel message to the audience, keynote of the Christian doctrines, future judgment?

7) What spiritual work did Paul accomplish at Athens? How much is tallied in the record of Acts?[3]

[3]The New Testament does not record any further visit of Paul to Athens. We have no epistle of Paul to the Athenians, and history bears out that the Christian community there slowly evaporated during the next hundred years before its reappearance. However, fruits of the gospel are of various species. Who can truly measure, for example, the full impact on all succeeding gen-

Corinth (18:1-17)

1) Analyze the various statements made by the Lord in Paul's vision.

2) Note the various ways Luke describes Paul's ministries.

3) What does this passage teach about the will of God? About His providence?

4) What is implied by the words, "Paul began devoting himself completely to the word" (18:5)?

5) What is implied by the words, "Do not be afraid any longer" (18:9)?

EXPLANATIONS

1) "Sharp disagreement" (15:39). The Greek word is *paroxusmos*, from which comes our intense word "paroxysm." (Cf. 17:16, where the word "provoked" translates the same Greek word.) Luke blames no one, though the friction was not of God. The solution of Barnabas and Paul parting ways was wise, for Barnabas, "son of encouragement," could help Mark develop into a stronger believer, and Paul could maintain the momentum of the first journey. The eventual outcome, resulting from the reconciling catalysis of forgiveness, was happy and blessed. There were two gospel ministries instead of one, and Mark was restored into a fruitful relationship with Paul as one of his fellow servants (Col. 4:10; Philemon 24; II Tim. 4:11). This is the last reference to Barnabas in Acts.[4]

2) "Spirit of Jesus" (16:7). The Holy Spirit.

3) "We" (16:10). This begins the first of the "we" sections of Acts, when Luke identifies himself as part of Paul's party. It has been suggested that Luke joined Paul at this time to administer medical help for an infirmity of the apostle. Luke remained with Paul as far as Philippi. He stayed in that city while Paul's party moved on; he joined the apostle again in the account of Acts 20:5.

erations of Paul's speech to the Areopagus, wherein is shown "the language which the Gospel addresses to a man on his proudest eminence of unaided strength"? W. J. Conybeare and J. S. Howson, *The Life and Epistles of St. Paul* (Grand Rapids: Wm. B. Eerdmans Publishing Co., 1950), p. 296.

[4]Reconciliation between Paul and Barnabas was also no doubt effected. Read I Cor. 9:6 for the one later reference to Barnabas by Paul.

4) "Marketplace" (17:17). This was the Agora, located to the west of the Acropolis. It was the hub of the life and activity of Athens.

5) "Very religious in all respects" (17:22). Opinion is divided as to whether Paul wanted to commend the Athenians for their religious inclinations, or whether he wanted to expose their sin at the very outset of his sermon as being "too religious" (a possible translation). What do you think?

6) "Overlooked the times of ignorance" (17:30). This is not a reference to God disregarding or thinking lightly of sin, but to His long-suffering and compassion in withholding judgment until the hour of the Son of Man. Of this G. Campbell Morgan writes: "A new hour had struck on the horologue of eternity, and men in time were arrested, for a new day had dawned."[5]

7) "He was of the same trade" (18:3). Tent making was a trade of little esteem and poor pay. (Read Paul's references to this in 20:34; I Cor. 9:7-12; II Cor. 11:7-9; I Thess. 2:9; II Thess. 3:8.)

8) "A year and six months" (18:11). Paul probably wrote I and II Thessalonians during this time.

9) "Judgment-seat" (18:12). This was the tribunal court, set up outdoors.

10) "Contrary to the law" (18:13). The Roman law forbade the propagation of an unauthorized religion. Judaism, a legal religion, enjoyed freedom as a religion per se, although the Roman authorities (e.g., Claudius) restricted freedom in individual cases. The objection of the Jews at Corinth was that Paul's religion was illegal because it did not fly the banner of Judaism. Gallio saw the problem as one of semantics ("questions about words and names," 18:15), and dismissed the charges.

11) "And he drove them away" (18:16). Gallio's precedent-making refusal to indict Paul was a bright moment for the evangelistic crusade, giving hopeful prospects for the future. Bruce says, "It meant that for the next ten or twelve years, until imperial policy towards the Christians underwent a complete reversal 'at the highest level' [around A.D. 64], the Christian mes-

[5]G. Campbell Morgan, *The Acts of the Apostles* (New York: Fleming H. Revell Co., 1924), p. 423.

sage could be proclaimed in the provinces of the empire without fear of coming into conflict with the Roman law."[6]

12) "Greeted the church" (18:22). The Jerusalem church must be intended here, for (1) Paul would hardly come this near the city without visiting the brethren there; and (2) the geographical description fits Jerusalem: going up to Jerusalem, and then down to Antioch. Whatever Paul did at Jerusalem was of brief duration; Luke sums it up by the word "greeted."

FURTHER ADVANCED STUDY

1) To better understand the lives of the people whom Paul led to Christ at Philippi and Thessalonica, read Philippians and I and II Thessalonians. The letters to the Thessalonians were written from Corinth soon after Paul had left Thessalonica. Philippians was written later when Paul was in prison at Rome.

2) Evaluate the apologetic method of teaching theism before preaching evangelistically to a group such as Paul faced on Mars Hill. How would such a method be appropriate on a college campus?

3) Compare Romans 1:18-25 with Paul's sermon at Athens.

4) What part does Athens play in the remainder of the New Testament, following Paul's mission there?

5) For outside reading on the subject of Athenian-type religion and philosophy, read chapters 5–7 of Wilbur M. Smith's *Therefore Stand*.

6) Read I and II Corinthians for further insight on the Corinthians.

7) Beginning with Paul's first missionary journey, make a comparative study of Paul's ministries to Jews and to Gentiles. Consider such items as time spent with, opposition by, and fruits from each group. After you have finished your survey of the third missionary journey, extend this study to include that mission.

WORDS TO PONDER

"I have many people in this city" (18:10).

---

[6]F. F. Bruce, *Commentary on the Book of Acts* (Grand Rapids: Wm. B. Eerdmans Publishing Co., 1954), pp. 375-76.

LESSON 21

THIRD MISSIONARY JOURNEY

18:23—21:17

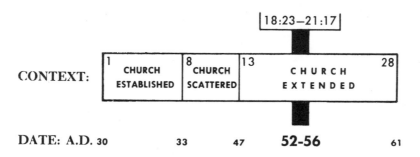

| 18:23—21:17 | | | | |

CONTEXT:

| 1 CHURCH ESTABLISHED | 8 CHURCH SCATTERED | 13 CHURCH EXTENDED 28 |

DATE: A.D. 30   33   47   **52-56**   61

PLACES: 4,000 mile journey (see map)

RULERS: Roman Emperors: Claudius (A.D. 41-54)
Nero (A.D. 54-68)
Proconsul of Asia: Marcus Junius Silanus (d. A.D. 54)

INTRODUCTION

THE END of Paul's second journey and the beginning of his third are so briefly and casually recorded by Luke that the reader of Acts is hardly aware that a new missionary crusade has begun. The second journey closes at 18:22, and in the very next verse,[1] though a period of time is spent at Antioch, Paul is off to the work again, moving about Galatia and Phrygia.

Luke's mingling of the terminus of one and the commencement of the other may suggest a compelling momentum which Paul preserved until this phase of his evangelistic ministry was

[1]The Berkeley Version accurately makes a new paragraph at 18:23, indicating the third journey's commencement here.

199

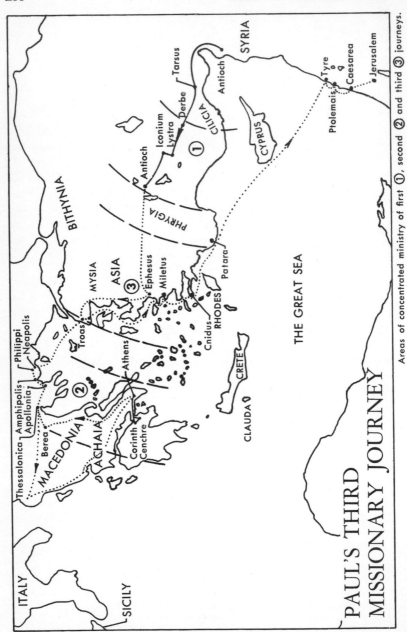

PAUL'S THIRD
MISSIONARY JOURNEY

Areas of concentrated ministry of first ①, second ② and third ③ journeys.

completed. Paul had greeted the Jerusalem church, and then had given a report of his work to the Antioch church. But after fulfilling those obligations he was on his way again. At this junction Paul must have known he was past the midpoint of this phase of the evangelistic program, and he already had Rome in his future plans (read 19:21). So there was one compelling drive —to get the work done while it was day. The season was favorable for travel and there was no hindrance by the Holy Spirit, so he departed for the third time from his friends and supporters at Antioch.

PREPARATION FOR STUDY

1) The passage 18:23—21:17 may be divided into the following segments for analytical study: 18:24—19:20[2]; 19:23-41; 20:1-12; 20:17-38; 21:1-17. The first and last segments are especially recommended for analytical chart work.

2) It will not be difficult for you to see the main objective of the third missionary journey when you observe on a map what important geographical area had been bypassed on Paul's second tour. Study the map at the beginning of this lesson and observe how the entire general region of Asia, with Ephesus as its capital, awaited a concentrated ministry of the gospel. Remember that the province of Asia and its capital city were more populous, wealthy and important than the provinces of Macedonia and Achaia and their cities.

3) Use a Bible dictionary to acquaint yourself with the following names associated with this last journey: People: Erastus, Demetrius, Artemis, Gaius, Aristarchus, Asiarchs, Alexander, Eutychus, Philip, Agabus, Mnason. Places: Miletus, Tyre, Ptolemais, Caesarea.

SURVEY OF THIRD MISSIONARY JOURNEY

First, read 18:23—21:17 in one sitting, noting places and persons of the narrative. On your second reading notice all the places where the action changes and whether the change is one of geography, action, personnel. Record this paragraph-to-para-

[2]The verse 18:23 does not form a natural part of this segment.

graph sequence on a horizontal survey chart. Now look for groupings of paragraphs and outline the passage.

Having made your own survey outline of this third journey, compare it with the outline shown on page 204. Note that this journey, like the other two, has three main parts or missions, which might be identified thus:

Mission A: This mission begins with a follow-up work in the general areas of Galatia and Phrygia, but the main ministry is at Ephesus. About three years were spent here (read 20:31).

Mission B: This mission aimed mainly at follow-up work in the churches of Macedonia and Achaia which Paul had evangelized on the second journey. This mission may have lasted from ten to fourteen months. It was a very busy mission, though only six verses of Acts are devoted to it. Paul writes more details in II Corinthians, from which the following sequence of events may be culled:

1) Leaving Ephesus in deep distress, Paul went to Troas 1:8; 2:12).

2) Brief evangelistic work at Troas; thence to Macedonia (2:12-13).

3) While Paul was experiencing affliction at Macedonia, Titus arrived with good news about the Corinthian church (7:5-16).

4) Paul then wrote II Corinthians, and sent it to Corinth with Titus and two other brethren (8:6, 16-22).

5) Follow-up ministry in other cities, where he also was gathering a collection for the poor of the Jerusalem church, which he had previously written about (cf. I Cor. 16:1-4). Also at this time Paul may have done a little pioneer evangelistic work in or near the province of Illyricum (northwest of Macedonia) (Rom. 15:19).

6) At Corinth Paul lodged with Gaius (Rom. 16:23), remaining there three months. Here he wrote his letter to the Christians at Rome (epistle to the Romans).

Mission C: This was the concluding return ministry, with short visits at places like Troas, Miletus and Caesarea.

Now read the passage of Acts a third time, recording those items of the narrative required in the survey chart on page 204.

QUESTIONS ON THE THIRD JOURNEY AND THE THREE JOURNEYS AS A WHOLE

1) What was the main objective of Paul's third journey? Was it accomplished?

2) What indications are there from the text that practically all of the province of Asia was evangelized on the third journey? Locate the cities named in Revelation 2–3 and also Colossae (Paul later wrote Colossians to the Christians there) and Hierapolis (Col. 4:13) on a map. The churches of these cities probably were founded during this crusade.

3) Compare the following aspects of this journey with those of the first two journeys:

   a) Paul's ministry to Jews; to Gentiles
   b) Paul's message
   c) Paul's follow-up ministry
   d) Miracles by Paul. Explain the "extraordinary" miracles at Ephesus (19:11).

4) Despite ill omens, Paul was determined to go to Jerusalem at the end of this trip. Luke gives no reasons for Paul's determination (except for the reference at 24:17). Read the following passages and conclude whether the collection for the poor was Paul's sole motive: I Corinthians 16:1ff; II Corinthians 8:1ff; Romans 15:25ff.

5) How much of Asia Minor,[3] Macedonia and Achaia was given a witness of the gospel by Paul and his missionary party during the course of the three crusades? On what would Paul depend for the continued spiritual nurture of the new local churches scattered throughout the provinces?

6) If Paul had been allowed another crusade before going to Rome, where do you think he might have wanted to go?

7) From what you know of the experiences of Paul on these

[3]It is noteworthy that there were about 230 communities of Asia Minor at this time. See E. M. Blaiklock, *The Acts of the Apostles* (Grand Rapids: Wm. B. Eerdmans Publishing Co., 1959), p. 154.

THIRD MISSIONARY JOURNEY
Acts 18:23—21:17

18:23	18:24	19:1	19:8	19:21	20:1		20:7	20:13	20:17	21:1	21:17
Galatia & Phrygia	Apollos	Paul to Ephesus	Teaching & Preaching	Riot	Macedonia & Greece		Troas	To Miletus	Farewell	To Jerusalem	
Galatia & Phrygia	Ephesus				Macedonia & Greece		Troas to Jerusalem				
MISSION (A)					MISSION (B)		MISSION (C)				
Follow-up	**NEW**				Follow-up		**CONCLUDING**				
about 3 years					10-14 months						
PERSONNEL											
DURATION											
ITINERARY DETERMINANTS											
MINISTRIES	I Cor. written				II Cor. written from Macedonia Romans written from Corinth						
KEY MESSAGES											
OPPOSITION & DELIVERANCE											
SIGNS & MIRACLES											
SPIRITUAL FRUIT											
KEY VERSES											

three journeys, compare the Paul who left Antioch for his first journey (13:3) with the Paul who walked into Jerusalem ten years later (21:17). What part did each of the following play in molding Paul's character?

   a) experiences with people
   b) communion with God
   c) fellowship with the saints
   d) growing knowledge of the Word.

8) What are your views on these questions: Was Paul right in rejecting John Mark's services? In taking a vow? In walking into the jaws of the opposition at Jerusalem? Justify your answers.

9) Some say one of Luke's purposes in Acts was to defend the peaceable intentions of Christians with respect to the empire, in anticipation of the false accusations against Christians which would originate with the imperial throne. If this was true, how would his record of Paul's journey serve that apologetic motive?

10) In tracing the progress of the Gentile mission of the early church in Acts, it has been pointed out that the geographical center of the mission kept moving—from the church at Jerusalem, to Antioch, to Ephesus, to Rome. If it was true that Ephesus replaced Antioch[4] as of this third journey, what were her qualifications?

11) From your study of Paul's farewell to the Ephesians (20: 17-38), list spiritual lessons taught in these areas: perseverance in service, Christian fellowship, purpose and goals, the crucified life, Satanic opposition.

EXPLANATIONS

1) "Upper country" (19:1). From the region of Phrygia to Ephesus there were two possible routes: (1) the direct route from the north, over a higher-lying road, and (2) the trade route on the lower elevations, passing through such valley cities as Colossae and Laodicea. Paul chose the upper route.

2) "The theater" (19:29). This was a large open-air theater with a capacity of at least 25,000 people.

---

[4]You have already observed that Paul never reached Antioch at the end of this third journey, though it may have been his original intention to do so.

3) "Waiting for us" (20:5). At this point Luke, having remained at Philippi while Paul and his party moved on (chapter
16), returns as a participant in the story of Acts. A suggestion
has been made that the "we" of Luke includes Titus also; that
Luke and Titus may have been brothers; and that all of this
partly explains why Luke refrained from writing about his own
brother in Acts.

4) "On the first day of the week" (20:7). Two earlier references to the "first day" are made in the New Testament at John
20:19 (cf. also v. 26) and I Corinthians 16:2. In the latter passage
at least there is a strong indication that the church was observing
this day in a special way. The present Acts passage is the first
explicit record of worship on that day.

5) "Will see my face no more" (20:25). Paul's statement was
not inspired prophecy but his own personal expectation. Very
likely Paul saw Ephesus again after his first Roman imprisonment. (Cf. Philemon 22, written from Rome, and I Tim. 1:3;
3:14, written after imprisonment.)

6) "Savage wolves" (20:29). Paul realistically forewarned the
Ephesian church of what he knew would happen after he left:
ravaging from without, seduction from within. When Paul later
wrote to Timothy, who then was pastoring the church of Ephesus, he referred to some of these problems. Read I Timothy
1:19-20; 4:1; II Timothy 2:17-18; 3:1-9; Revelation 2:1-7.

7) "The words of the Lord Jesus" (20:35). The saying of
Jesus which Paul quoted is not in the New Testament, though
the spirit of the maxim is found in such verses as Luke 6:38. A
collection of Jesus' sayings was probably in circulation at this
time.

FURTHER ADVANCED STUDY

1) Read Paul's letter to the Ephesians, written at a later date,
to discover some insights into the lives of the believers of the
church of Ephesus. At some later time Paul appointed his under-
study, Timothy, to pastor the church at Ephesus. Read Paul's
two letters to Timothy, written at different times, to learn of some
of the problems and tasks of the young minister in this large
congregation.

2) Inquire further into the differences between the baptism by John the Baptist and baptism in the name of Jesus. The Gospels and Epistles supplement Acts on this subject.

3) What salutary function should "fear of God" play in the heart of an unbeliever? What kind of fear should the Christian overcome? What kind of fear is he commanded to have? (See references to such fear in Peter's first epistle.)

4) In this passage is the New Testament's first explicit reference to Sunday worship by the Christian church. From church history and the Bible make a defense of the observance of Sunday as the holy day of the week, and show its relation to the Old Testament Sabbath. What are the basic principles common to Sabbath and Sunday observance?

5) This passage no doubt has caused you to think more about the subject "How can I know the will of God?" Cite answers to the question from the Bible.

6) When Paul entered Jerusalem, he knew he was a marked man. He needed to depend on God's protection if he was to survive. Study the subject of the providence of God, with this as a starting point.

7) The Lord's Supper was one of the important observances in the worship service of the early Christians. Study these areas of this important subject: The gospel's teaching about the Lord's Supper; the observances in Acts and in early church history; the relationship of the Agape (love) feast to the Lord's Supper; the church's observance of the Lord's Supper today.

8) Repentance and faith are requisites for conversion. Notice how the two are related in 20:21. Make a study of this relationship as it is taught in other places in the New Testament.

WORDS TO PONDER
"Being fervent in spirit" (18:25).

PAUL BEFORE THE MOB AND COUNCIL

21:18—23:30

		21:18–23:30	

CONTEXT:

1 CHURCH ESTABLISHED	8 CHURCH SCATTERED	13 CHURCH EXTENDED	28

DATE: A.D. 30   33   47   **56**   61

PLACES: Jerusalem: temple; barracks, council chamber

RULERS: Emperor: Nero
Governor of Judea: Felix (A.D. 52-58)
Tetrarch of Chalcis and other northern territory: King Agrippa (Herod II) (A.D. 48-70)

INTRODUCTION

LUKE HAD JUST one more large section of Paul's apostolic ministry to record before closing his account of Acts. Luke knew he was not writing a complete biography of Paul, so any awareness that Paul might be given later opportunity to serve God in even greater ministries did not deter him from closing his account where he did. Borne of the Holy Spirit, the physician-author designed Acts to close with an action-packed account of the appearances of Paul the prisoner in defense of his witness-appearances before an angry mob, a disorganized council, and confused rulers—all of this leading to his finally reaching Rome, the goal of his heart.

Your study in this lesson is twofold: first, to make a survey of this entire last section of Acts, and then to study more closely the passages 21:18—22:29 and 22:30—23:30.

I. SURVEY OF 21:18—28:31

Your original survey of Acts included a brief look at these chapters so that you could see their relation to the preceding events. Now, in anticipation of analyzing the smaller segments of this section, try to get an overall view of the section to determine relationships between the segments.

Do not refer to the accompanying survey chart until you have made your own survey study. Draw a horizontal line on a sheet of paper and record the following division references:

21:18	22:30	23:31	25:1	25:13	27:1	28:31

Next, read each small section to determine its major content; then record this. Then begin to look for groupings of sections, about such subjects as geography, people Paul encountered, and experiences of Paul. Look also for any progressions or turning points. Compare the beginning and ending of the section. By doing all this you will form an overall view of the last chapters of Acts.

The accompanying survey chart of 21:18—28:31 is given for you to make comparisons with your own survey, and to identify the organization of Lessons 26—29 of the manual.

II. STUDY OF 21:18—22:29

Paul in the Hands of the Mob

Study this passage in these four parts:

A. Anticipation of Conflict	21:18-26
B. Paul Attacked	21:27-36
C. Paul's Defense	21:37—22:21
D. Outcome	22:22-29

APPEARANCES OF PAUL THE PRISONER
Acts 21:18—28:31

CLAMOR OF MOB VIOLENCE

CALM OF FRIENDLY GATHERINGS

21:18	22:30	23:31	25:1	25:13	27:1	28:31
Before the Mob	Before the Council	Before the Governors		Before the King		Before Jews and with Visitors
		Felix	Festus	Agrippa		

Paul's Defenses:

22:1-21	23:1, 3, 6	24:10b-21	25:8, 10, 11	26:2-23; 25-27, 29		28:17-20; 23-31

ACCUSED BY THE JEWS	ABSOLVED BY THE RULERS	AWAITING TRIAL
At Jerusalem	At Caesarea	To Rome
Lesson 26	Lesson 27 Lesson 28	Lesson 29

KEY

Paul: Innocent (23:1)
God: Protector (23:11)
Work: Waiting (23:11)

GOSPEL MINISTER ATTACKED

GOSPEL MINISTER UNHINDERED

After you have read the entire passage in one sitting, approach each part individually, using the following questions and suggestions.

A. *Anticipation of Conflict* (21:18-26)

1) When Paul reached Jerusalem it was Pentecost time, with thousands of Jews from far and near crowding the streets and temple area. The issue over the relationship of Jew and Gentile was still a live and sensitive one. What basically was involved here?

2) What was the elders' attitude concerning the Gentile mission?

3) Was it for the thousands of Jewish believers or for the Jewish unbelievers that the recommendation of 21:24 was given? As it turned out, who were the troublemakers? (cf. 21:27-28, 30).

4) Explain Luke's silence concerning the offering for the saints which Paul and his brethren brought to the Jerusalem church (cf. 21:17; 24:17).

5) Do you think Paul acted wisely in participating in the vow ceremonies? In answering this, consider such questions as:

   a) Was Paul consistent with his own teaching? (cf. I Cor. 9:20). Was he compromising?

   b) Can you tell from the account whether his participation was effective? What good might have been accomplished? Consider the following comment of the Berkeley version on Paul's action: "What grace on Paul's part to whom ritual had lost all virtue!"

B. *Paul Attacked* (21:27-36)

1) Observe the various references to physical violence against Paul.
2) Who initiated the riot? Who joined in?
3) What typical aspects of riot are recorded?
4) What accusations were brought against Paul? Why do you suppose the commander had him bound with chains?

C. *Paul's Defense* (21:37—22:21)

You may choose to analyze this segment by using an analytical chart. If so, the five paragraph divisions should be as follows: 21:37; 22:1, 6, 12, 17. This passage contains many wonderful things for an analytical study.

Paul was wise in his courteous relations with the commander as he sought an opportunity to speak to the people. The "great hush" which fell over the hitherto screaming mobs was a miracle of God intended to electrify the words of Paul's moving personal testimony. Added to the effect of the hush was the warm gesture of the salutation "Brethren and fathers" and the vernacular Aramaic used by Paul, so that the people "became even more quiet"! (22:2). In all his ministry Paul probably never commanded more rapt attention than this.

Luke narrated Paul's conversion experience earlier in Acts. The unique value of this present account[1] is that we have in Paul's own words the apostle's reflections on the highlights of his life, as he personally evaluated them in their context.[2] Notice that the testimony Paul gave concerns four such highlights:

1. Preconversion years   22:3-5
2. Conversion day   22:6-11
3. General ministry appointed   22:12-16
4. Special mission identified   22:17-21

Analyze each of the above four paragraphs and try to determine how Paul's different statements were geared to the audience. Observe how clearly Paul understood his need for salvation, his conversion and his call. Observe also the emphasis he places on God and the doctrine of the resurrection in his various experiences.

Paul's testimony begins with "I am a Jew" and ends with "Go! . . . to the Gentiles." He was born a Jew; that was ordained of God. He was sent to Gentiles; that was of God. If the mobs wanted to kill him for this, they must answer to God.

---

[1]Paul gives another similar personal testimony in 26:2-23.
[2]Paul's original speech probably was somewhat wordier than what Luke includes here, but the emphases and highlights are nevertheless preserved.

D. *Outcome* (22:22-29)

The mobs *did* want to kill Paul: "He should not be allowed to live!" (22:22). Why did the commander order Paul to be scourged? As of this time has Paul been officially condemned for any crime? Why should there be hesitation on the part of the commander to release Paul at this time?

APPLICATIONS

1) What sins of the heart underlie opposition to the gospel ministry?

2) How should a Christian act in the face of falsehood and rumor against him?

3) How should a Christian act in persecution? What should constitute the scope of his testimony? Should human rights be claimed? How much dependence should he have on God?

4) About what things in his life and service for God should a Christian have clear understanding and strong conviction?

5) What do you learn from this passage about Christian grace, perseverance, spiritual strength?

6) List other important lessons taught here.

III. STUDY OF 22:30—23:30

Paul Before the Council

Read 22:30 and observe how this verse acts as a connector between what has gone before—Paul in the hands of the mob— and what follows—Paul before the council (Sanhedrin). The commander did not have a clear case brought against Paul by the Jewish mob; his quick strategy to extract the truth by scourging had failed; now he sought light from the astute assembly of the council. But he was to fail here as well, and was finally driven to refer Paul to the governor.

Read through this passage a few times, observing the variety of situations Paul encountered. Divide the passage into the following four paragraphs, and answer the questions given below:

      A. Paul and the Council   (22:30—23:10)
      B. Paul and the Lord   (23:11)

C. Paul and his Nephew   (23:12-22)
D. Paul and the Letter   (23:23-30)

QUESTIONS

1) What are the different strategies against Paul recorded here?

2) What reasons do the first, second and last paragraphs give for Paul's arrest and trial?

3) Observe how Paul is given help in the experience of each paragraph. Distinguish between direct and indirect help.

4) 22:30—23:10. Account for Ananias' action of 23:2 and Paul's words of 23:3. Was Paul speaking truthfully in verse 5a? What was Paul's real motive in speaking the words of 6b?

5) 23:11. In what different ways would these words help Paul at this time? What light do the words throw on Paul's Jerusalem visit, and his Rome ministry?

6) Look for spiritual applications from this passage. For example, what is learned here of the helping hand of the Lord?

EXPLANATIONS

1) "Commander of the Roman Cohort" (21:31). A cohort consisted of a thousand soldiers, hence the title of their leader was "chiliarch" (Greek *chiliarchos*, "commander of a thousand"). NASB translates the word as "commander"; RSV, "tribune"; AV, "chief captain." This cohort garrisoned the large building called the Tower of Antonia which was located in the northwest corner of the temple and accessible to the courts by stairs (cf. 21:35). The commander used a few hundred of his soldiers to quell the riot. The commander's name was Claudius Lysias (23:26).

2) "Hebrew dialect" (21:40). Now Paul wisely resorts to the Aramaic vernacular, the Hebrew dialect of the Jews. (Hebrew at this time was not the common language of the Jews; it was used only in the temple and synagogue services.)

3) "Trance" (22:17). Compare Mark 5:42; 16:8; Luke 5:26; Acts 3:10; 10:10; 11:5.

4) "Lord, they themselves understand . . ." (22:19). Paul's reasoning was that the big transformation in the direction of his zeal would attest to the sincerity of his testimony.

5) "Find out the reason why they were shouting against him" (22:24). The Roman commander had not understood Paul's Aramaic speech.

6) "Examined by scourging" (22:24). Read a description of scourging in a Bible dictionary.

7) "I acquired this citizenship . . . money" (22:28). Roman citizenship was acquired in any of three ways: (1) by birth, of parents who were Roman citizens (Paul); (2) by money (commander); and (3) as a gift by the Roman government—to honor the recipient or to reward one for meritorious service (one of Paul's ancestors probably acquired citizenship this way).

8) "High priest Ananias" (23:2). Ananias was high priest from A.D. 47 to 48, during which time he utterly profaned the sacred office with a life of greed, fraud, violence and self-glory. He was eventually assassinated in A.D. 66.

9) "I was not aware" (23:5). Three possible explanations of Paul's answer to the bystanders are:

a) This not being a regular meeting of the council, the high priest, whom Paul would not recognize by face,[3] was not sitting in his usual place, nor wearing his regular official robes.

b) Paul miscalculated from where the words issued, thinking another member of the council had spoken them.

c) Paul spoke the words in irony, meaning in effect, "I did not know that a man acting this way was the high priest."

10) "Son of Paul's sister" (23:16). Nothing more is known of Paul's sister and nephew. In view of Paul's conversion to Christ, it is an interesting exercise to speculate about the relationship of his parents and other members of his family to the apostle. Might Paul have been disowned? Did Paul have the experience of leading any of his family to Christ? Neither Luke nor Paul write any detail about the apostle's family relationships before or after his conversion.

[3]Paul was literally a stranger to Jerusalem by this time, having been "on the road" for most of the past twenty years.

FURTHER ADVANCED STUDY

1) Compare the three records in Acts of Paul's conversion: Luke's account (9:1-19a); two personal testimonies of Paul (22:4-16; 26:12-18). Observe the likenesses and differences. What does Luke make prominent? What does Paul emphasize? (For outside reading on the comparison of the three conversion accounts, consult Goodwin, *op. cit.*, pp. 199-202.)

2) It is noteworthy that the New Testament does not give any detailed information on the two punishments of scourging and crucifixion. Read outside sources on these cruel practices, observing the unjust procedures of law accompanying them.

WORDS TO PONDER

"I will send you far away . . ." (22:21).

PAUL BEFORE THE GOVERNORS

23:31—25:12

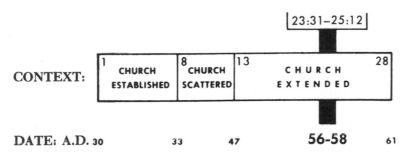

23:31-25:12		

CONTEXT:

1 CHURCH ESTABLISHED	8 CHURCH SCATTERED	13 CHURCH EXTENDED 28

DATE: A.D. 30   33   47   **56-58**   61

PLACES: Caesarea: governor's official residence; prison; tribunal meeting place. Also Jerusalem.

RULERS: Governors of Judea: Felix (A.D. 52-58)
                        Porcius Festus (A.D. 58-61)

INTRODUCTION

PAUL'S INCREASING UNEASINESS about the safety of his life is understandable. It was with reckless abandon that he was being "shoved" from one hearing to another, while the cause of his arrest became increasingly more confused to his inquisitors. Except for the Lord's word of hope (23:11), he could have expected conviction at any time. The plot to kill Paul was reason enough for the Roman commander at Jerusalem to snatch the apostle out of the city and to send him to the higher Roman authority, the governor of Judea, who resided in Caesarea. Paul must have meditated long over the prospects of such a confrontation as he

217

rode on horseback in the large company of Roman soldiers to the
seacoast city.

PREPARATION FOR STUDY

1) Review all that has transpired since the Asian Jews first
stirred up the multitudes in the temple (21:27). The accompanying diagram shows how Paul was almost referred back to the
Jewish contingent of Jerusalem, reviving the confusion from which
he had recently been delivered. (Follow the order A, B, C.) In
your own review of these chapters pick out other highlights that
suggest various aspects of Paul's appearances as a prisoner.

DISPOSITION OF PAUL THE PRISONER

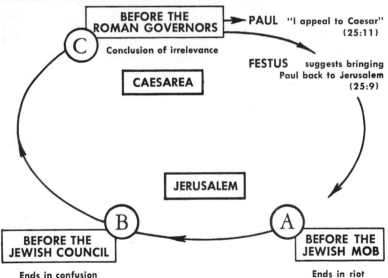

2) Make a list of the actual charges made against Paul as Luke
records these from time to time in the section 21:18–26:32.

3) Try to imagine the many things Paul would be thinking
about on his way to Caesarea from Jerusalem. Look at a map of
Palestine (showing topography and roads) and speculate on the
route the contingent may have taken.

4) Read 23:25-35 just before you begin your study of chapter
24.

ANALYSIS

I. BEFORE FELIX (24:1-27)

Antonius Felix was governor of Judea from A.D. 52 to 58, a period of time when the peace was challenged by uprisings and insurrections which he managed to suppress, though ruthlessly. When Paul was brought to him, he was already feeling the opposition and discontent of various groups of moderate Jews throughout the province over his radical administration. To hear of another riot in Jerusalem was unwelcome news to his ears.

1) Divide this chapter into three main paragraphs, with the divisions at verses 1, 10 and 22. As you read through the chapter the first time, you should have no difficulty justifying each paragraph as a unit of thought.

2) Observe the marginal note in NASB for verses 6 and 7.

3) After you have read through the passage at least twice, begin to gather your observations and record them on your analytical chart. As in previous lessons, suggestions for study are given below the accompanying skeleton chart.

4) Observe the frequency of negatives in the first part of Paul's defense, followed by the positives of his testimony in the latter half. Also contrast the details of Paul's defense with the generalities of Tertullus' speech.

5) Study the four words *Way, serve, hope* and *conscience* as they are joined together by Paul in his testimony (verses 14-16). Relate these to Christian living today.

6) How much light of the gospel did Felix have? Suggest some of the things which he and Drusilla (his third wife) might have mentioned in their discussions with Paul on the subjects of righteousness, self-control and judgment to come. How pertinent were such subjects to Felix and Drusilla?

7) What kept Felix from becoming a believer? Keep in mind the growing unpopularity of Felix in his office as governor. Observe that the governor was faced with two options, as different as black from white:

THIS	OR THIS
—favor Paul (by releasing him)	—favor the accusing Jews (by condemning Paul)
—incur further unpopularity	—gain more friends
—resolve a spiritual issue (of his soul)	—resolve a secular problem (of his office)

Are his sins of verses 25-27 common today?

II. BEFORE FESTUS (25:1-12)

Felix was unable to stem the tide of internal problems of dissension over his maintaining peace in the land, and two years after Paul's first appearance before him he was recalled to Rome, and replaced by Porcius Festus.[1]

Reconstruct in your mind the new situation confronting Paul, involving such things as:

1) Festus' desire to begin his reign in the favor of the multitudes
2) Festus not being acquainted yet with the facts of Paul's case
3) A festering tendency endangering a case of this sort which has been shelved for such a long period
4) Festus being a novice in office, vulnerable to exploitation

Compare Festus' own account of these events given later to Agrippa (25:14-21).

Observe that Luke's story revolves about three different suggestions made concerning Paul:

1) By the Jewish accusers: Bring Paul to Jerusalem
2) By Festus to Jews: Come to Caesarea and prosecute Paul there
3) By Festus to Paul: Will you go up to Jerusalem?

In the light of this context in which subtle maneuvers and plots were involved, how crucial and pivotal were Paul's words, "I appeal to Caesar"?

From the text of these twelve verses you should draw vital spiritual lessons about the subtle and devious ways of Satan to

[1]Festus' rule was brief, lasting only from A.D. 58 to 61.

Acts 24:1-27

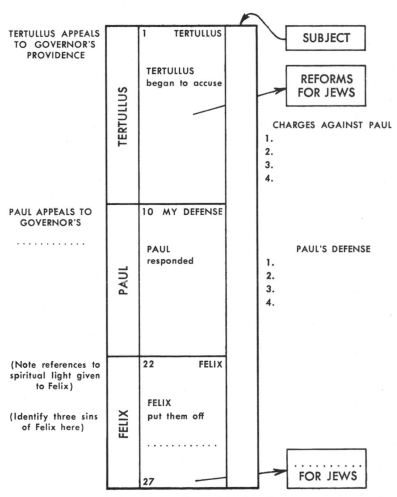

1. Block off the speeches of Tertullus and Paul in the respective paragraphs.
2. Identify the main subject of each paragraph.
3. What four major charges against Paul does Tertullus cite?
4. How does Paul answer each charge?
5. What is the surrounding context of the subject of "resurrection"? (verse 15)
6. Compare the opening appeal of Paul and Tertullus to Felix.
7. Note references to Jews in each paragraph.

lure the workers of God to a place of impotency and ineffective-
ness. What New Testament verses come to your mind exhorting
Christians to watch this archenemy in such devices?

EXPLANATIONS

1) "When he learned that he was from Cilicia" (23:34). Felix
could officially rule on the case of a citizen of the Roman province
of Cilicia.

2) "Sect of the Nazarenes" (24:5). Since Jesus was referred
to as "the Nazarene," it was natural for His followers to be labeled
as a "sect of the Nazarenes." Compare 2:22.

3) "Judge to this nation" (24:10). In the native Jewish land
of Judea the Roman governor was truly the ruler (or judge) of
the Jews.

4) "His friends" (24:23). Recall who lived in Caesarea at this
time and could be a real source of encouragement to Paul.

5) "Drusilla" (24:24). This Jewess, daughter of Herod Agrippa I, was not yet twenty years of age at this time. Felix was her
second husband; she was Felix's third wife.

6) "Self-control" (24:25). The Berkeley Version translates this
"mastery of passions." Read the following verses for other appearances of the same Greek word: Galatians 5:23; II Peter 1:6;
I Corinthians 9:25; Titus 1:8.

7) "I appeal to Caesar" (25:11). Such an appeal to the emperor himself, the supreme court of Rome, was the legal right of
Roman citizens at any stage of their trial. Nero, who was emperor at the time, had not yet launched his devastating antichristian crusade. Paul knew he would not receive justice in
Jerusalem; in Rome he at least could hope for it. Besides, here
was his opportunity to reach Rome, traveling under the empire's
auspices!

FURTHER ADVANCED STUDY

1) Paul makes a very clear statement of the resurrection of the
wicked dead in 24:15. His epistles make frequent references to
the resurrection of the believers (e.g., the classic chapter I Cor.
15), where that aspect of resurrection was the point of his mes-

sage. Make a study in the New Testament of the various references to the resurrection of the unbeliever, whether the reference is implicit or explicit. Include in your study John 5:28-29 and Revelation 20:12-13. For outside reading, consult: *The Doctrine of Eternal Punishment,* Harry Buis; *The Biblical Doctrine of Judgment,* Leon Morris; *The Future Life,* Rene Pache; *Prophecy for Today,* J. Dwight Pentecost.

2) Make a New Testament study of "temperance" or self-control as a manner of Christian living. How is temperance related to moderation?

3) One prominent aspect of Luke's narrative of Acts is the ever recurring confrontation of the apostles with civil authority. Answer the following questions with what you have observed in Acts:

a) Did the apostles ever resist civil authority?

b) To what extent did the apostles resist religious authority, even though its power was delegated from the state?

c) Verbally, what did the apostles assert as their highest authority? What price were they willing to pay for their allegiance?

d) What relationship did the apostles maintain with civil authority as to courtesy and obedience?

e) In this twentieth century, how should a Christian live under a government hostile to Christianity? What attitudes, convictions, knowledge and spiritual armor will prepare and reinforce Christians for trials and persecutions which may befall them?

WORDS TO PONDER

"When I find time" (24:25).

LESSON 24

PAUL BEFORE A KING

25:13—26:32

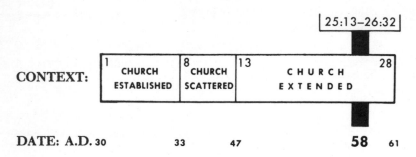

CONTEXT:

1	8	13	28
CHURCH ESTABLISHED	CHURCH SCATTERED	CHURCH EXTENDED	

25:13–26:32

DATE: A.D. 30   33   47   **58**   61

PLACES: Caesarea: auditorium

RULERS: King Herod Agrippa II, tetrarch of Chalcis and of northern territory (A.D. 48-70)
Governor Festus

INTRODUCTION

"YOU HAVE APPEALED TO CAESAR, to Caesar you shall go," said Festus to Paul. But when the governor was making preparations to send Paul to Rome, he realized he had no charges to write about in referring him to the emperor. At such a time as this King Agrippa (Herod Agrippa II) arrived with his sister Bernice from his kingdom[1] in the north, having come to officially salute Festus as new governor of Judea. Festus knew of Agrippa's

---

[1]Agrippa would have succeeded his father King Agrippa I (Herod of 12:1) to the throne of Judea at his father's death in A.D. 44, had he not been so young (seventeen). Instead he was given a small kingdom in Lebanon, which he later relinquished in exchange for a larger domain located in southern Syria (Iturea, Trachonitis and Abilene; cf. Luke 3:1). Later his domain was increased by the addition of a few cities in Galilee and Perea, and with responsibilities in connection with the temple treasury in Jerusalem and the appointment of the high priest.

knowledge of the Jewish religion,[2] and no doubt hoped the king could help him compose a logical letter of referral that would be acceptable to the emperor. Agrippa not only agreed to help; he asked to hear firsthand whatever Paul had to say in his own defense.

PREPARATION FOR STUDY

1) First read 25:13-27 and become thoroughly acquainted with the setting of the narrative. Observe the dominant atmosphere of the paragraph 25:23-27. Visualize the contrast between the regal robes and the prisoner's chains. What may have been Paul's reflections on the "great pomp"? (25:23).

2) Think over Festus' reference to "a certain dead man, Jesus, whom Paul asserted to be alive" (25:19). In the account thus far has Luke reported the Jews as talking about this? Has Paul said much about resurrection in referring to the charges against him?

3) To see better the testimony of Paul in its setting, study the survey of the passage 25:13–26:32 on page 226. Of all the appearances of Paul before his examiners, this one afforded the best opportunity for the apostle to speak to their hearts. His actual success cannot be fully determined, for Luke has recorded only the first of their reactions.

ANALYSIS (26:1-29)

1) The segment 26:1-29 may be divided into four paragraphs, as shown on the chart on page 228. Mark these paragraph divisions in your Bible text before you begin to read.

2) Read the passage through the first time for major impressions. As you read be aware of the clear presentations of the facts of the gospel which Paul makes in the course of his testimony. Read the passage the second time more slowly, underlining words and phrases which you will want to analyze more closely later.

3) Continue your study by following the procedure of the analytical chart method. In your textual re-creation you will probably need to omit some of the subordinate items because of lack of space. You will want to tarry long over your textual re-

[2]Agrippa apparently had a reputation as an expert in this field (26:2, 3).

PAUL'S SPEECH BEFORE AGRIPPA
Acts 25:13—26:32

25:13	25:23	26:1	26:24	26:30-32
FESTUS BRIEFS AGRIPPA	PAUL PRESENTED TO AGRIPPA	PAUL'S TESTIMONY AND DEFENSE	RESPONSES OF FESTUS AND AGRIPPA	RULERS' CONCLUSIONS

FESTUS' DILEMMA

At a loss how to investigate.   At a loss how to write the emperor.

Note: While Paul's speech is apologetic, the apostle in this hearing goes to great length to present a positive statement of his divine call and mission.[3] It was so spiritually oriented to the souls of his audience that a personal response was inevitable. Luke records such reactions of Festus and Agrippa.

PAUL'S INNOCENCE RECOGNIZED

[3]Notice that Paul makes direct reference to his trial or arrest in only four places during his speech of twenty-two verses (26:2-23).

creation of verses 16-18, which contain various truths beautifully interwoven. Be sure your chart places due emphasis on the primary truths spoken by Paul before Agrippa.

4) Verses 6-8 seem to cut into the chronological sequence of Paul's account of his life. How do you explain this?[4] (Is there any connection between "Pharisee" of verse 5 and the theme of resurrection in verses 6-8?)

5) The chart on page 228 suggests other studies in this passage which you will want to pursue now.

6) We are always interested in observing how the gospel message was received by unbelievers in New Testament days. How do you explain Festus' reaction? Let Paul's answer shed light on this question. What was Paul's purpose in asking Agrippa, "Do you believe the Prophets?" The answer of Agrippa is rather ambiguous of itself; notice how the alternate rendering of NASB gives a different twist. Study Paul's response (verse 29) for whatever help it may give on understanding the real intent of Agrippa's reply of verse 28. (Refer to EXPLANATIONS section for further discussion of this.)

7) Where and how does Paul refer to *resurrection* in his testimony?

8) Before leaving chapter 26, read verses 30-32. Recall Festus' original reason for bringing Paul before Agrippa (25:26-27). Does Festus have his wish?

9) The spiritual truths of this passage are of various kinds. Make a list of the prominent ones that you see. The list might include truths about salvation, works, conversion, call, service, obedience, endurance, the gospel message and passion for souls.

EXPLANATIONS

1) "Bernice" (25:13). Bernice, Drusilla (24:24) and the Agrippa of this verse (25:13) were the children of Herod Agrippa I.

2) "Auditorium" (25:23). This was the governor's audience chamber.

[4]The Berkeley Version relates verse 8 to 9 by translating the first words of verse 9 as "Fact is that I was possessed of the idea. . . ." Its footnote of explanation represents Paul as reasoning, "If he, the fanatic, could be so convinced, why not any other Jews?"

Acts 26:1-29

ATMOSPHERE:

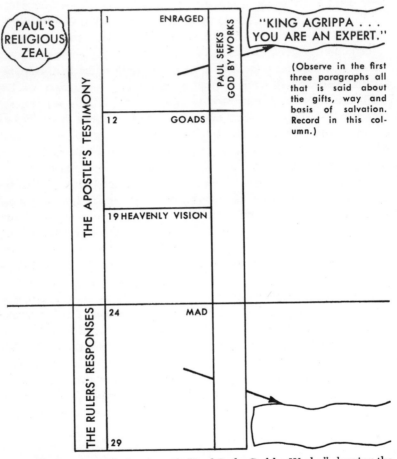

1. Complete the study begun with "Paul Seeks God by Works," showing the relationship of Paul to God in each paragraph.
2. Since most of this passage is a personal testimony, much is learned here of Paul. Make a paragraph-to-paragraph study of Paul, beginning with "Paul's Religious Zeal."
3. Compare Paul's opening words to Agrippa (shown above) with those spoken at the end. What is Paul's attitude in each situation?
4. Make a study of the "help of God" as shown throughout the passage. Look even for the implied references.
5. Observe the various atmospheres from beginning to end in this segment.

3) "It is hard for you to kick against the goads" (26:14). The word translated "hard" does not mean "difficult." RSV translates "It hurts you"; Berkeley, "It is hard on you." As oxen kicking against the proddings of goads, so Paul was resisting God's pricking his conscience, and the apostle was feeling the intensifying anguish of soul.

4) "In a short time you will persuade me to become a Christian" (26:28). There are various translations of this passage, because both the context and the Greek vocabulary allow for the differences.[5] Literally, the sentence reads, "In a little, you are persuading me to make a Christian." The options concern two parts of the verse:

a) "in a little": in a little time; or, in brief (with little)

b) "make": become; or, play the role of

If we knew Agrippa's motive, we would know what he meant by his words. Was he being sarcastic, "In a short time, you think to make me a Christian!"? (RSV.; cf. Wuest). Was he jesting when he said, "Much more of this, Paul, and you will be making me a Christian!" (Phillips)? Or was he being frank and blunt, implying that Paul was trying to get him to take an opposite side from Festus, "In short, you are trying to make me play the Christian" (Bruce; *New Bible Commentary*)? The fact that Agrippa brought in the word "Christian" (a word which Paul may not have used in his testimony[6]) suggests another angle of evil intent, for the word "Christian" in the mouth of a Jew had the bitter taste of contempt.

Whether Agrippa's intent was sincere, light or evil, Paul seized the first of the king's words and let them introduce the apostle not as a teacher of doctrines or defender of the gospel but as a man with a heart yearning to share his salvation—minus the chains —with others.

FURTHER ADVANCED STUDY

1) The sight of Stephen being stoned to death left no small impression on Saul the persecutor. Paul had a conscience, how-

[5]The Authorized version's "Almost thou persuadest me to be a Christian," based on the Byzantine text, is inaccurate.

[6]The speeches of Acts probably do not record every word originally spoken.

ever sensitive it was and by whatever standards it judged, and God used that conscience for His purposes. Make a topical study of "conscience" as the word appears in the Bible. Refer to outside works as well. Determine clearly in your mind the real functions of conscience. Recommended outside reading: *Conscience*, O. Hallesby; *The Voice of Conscience*, Alfred M. Rehwinkel; *Guilt and Grace*, Paul Tournier.

2) Make a cross-reference study of all the verses cited in the NASB margin in reference to 26:18. Note especially the Colossians passage and make comparisons.

3) "Great learning is driving you mad" (26:24). What are your views on learning and education? What should be the place of education in Christian living? What are the differences between Christian-oriented education and secular "neutral" education? Is there such a thing as a purely neutral starting point in one's learning about life's past origins, present experiences and future destinies?

WORDS TO PONDER

"I did not prove disobedient to the heavenly vision" (26:19).

LESSON 25

PAUL REACHES ROME

27:1—28:31

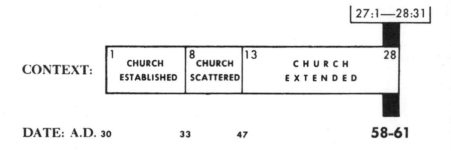

CONTEXT:

| 1 CHURCH ESTABLISHED | 8 CHURCH SCATTERED | 13 CHURCH EXTENDED | 28 |

27:1—28:31

DATE: A.D. 30   33   47   **58-61**

PLACES: 2,000 mile journey from Caesarea to Rome

RULER: Emperor Nero

INTRODUCTION

LUKE HAD ONE MORE CHAPTER of this part of Paul's life to write about—his journey to Rome and ministry there. Luke probably wrote the last verses of Acts at the end of the two full years of 28:30, that is, early in A.D. 61. Had his book been intended to contain a complete biography of Paul's life and Christian ministry, its project would have been delayed until after the apostle's death. But Acts was written with a larger purpose: to show the fulfillment of Christ's mandate-prophecy, "You shall be my witnesses . . . to the remotest part. . . ." Literally, the "remotest part" from Palestine would include places like India and China. But figuratively for the apostles it meant the extreme limits of *their* world, and their world was the Roman Empiré. When Luke

231

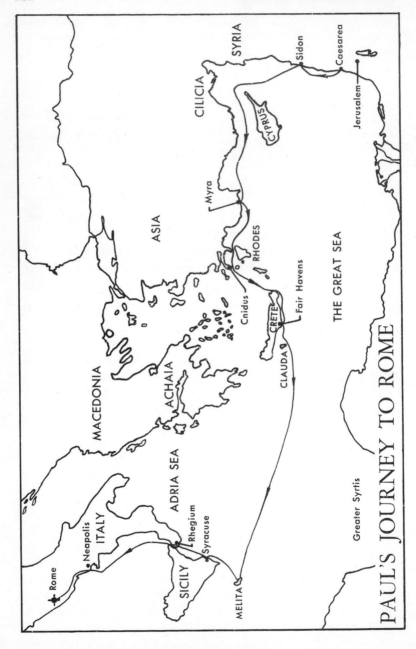

PAUL'S JOURNEY TO ROME

wrote Acts, the church in the person of the apostle had officially arrived as a witness to the empire's capital. There was nothing more for Luke to write.

PREPARATION FOR STUDY (28:14b-31)

1) In anticipation of analyzing the segment 28:14b-31, read 27:1—28:14a. This is the exciting detailed narrative of Paul's journey to Rome. Paul was an experienced sea traveler. Moreover, he already had participated in three shipwrecks (II Cor. 11:25), so he knew the potential dangers involved and how to survive. You will note from verses 1 and 2 that Luke and Aristarchus accompanied Paul on the journey. As you read the narrative, picture yourself as one of Paul's attendants.

As it turned out, Paul's journey was in four stages. Observe these divisions as you read the complete story:

a) Caesarea to Crete   (27:1-8)
b) Crete to Malta (shipwreck)   (27:9-44)
c) Stay at Malta   (28:1-10)
d) Malta to Rome   (28:11-14)

Be sure to trace the course of the journey in its various stages on a map, observing the strategy of their itinerary which Luke notes from time to time (e.g., "under the shelter of Cyprus because the winds were contrary," 27:4).[1] You may choose to consult a commentary on this portion in order to appreciate the many nautical terms and situations included in the story.

Observe the many spiritual truths this passage offers. What do you learn about Paul's character? About his influence? About obstacles and hindrances? About the supernatural—its timing, purposes and effects? Try reading the story as an allegory, likening Paul's journey experiences to a Christian's journey in life.

2) Review the references in Acts to Paul's going to Rome:

[1]Some seamanship references are not so obvious to the reader. For example, the statement "the voyage was now dangerous, since even the Fast was already over" (27:9) describes the plight that since it was now sometime in October (the month of the Day of Atonement—see NASB margin), the months November to January, in which navigation in the sea was forbidden by winter weather, were upon them.

19:21	"I must also see Rome"	(Paul)
23:11	"So you must witness at Rome also"	(the Lord)
25:12	"To Caesar you shall go"	(Festus)
27:24	"You must stand before Caesar"	(angel of God)
28:14	"And thus we came to Rome"	(Luke)

What do you suppose were Paul's feelings and expectations when he arrived in the city? James Stalker has offered an interesting suggestion:

> It was not with the step of a prisoner, but with that of a conqueror, that he passed at length beneath the city gate. His road lay along that very Sacred Way by which many a Roman general had passed in triumph to the Capitol, seated on a car of victory, followed by the prisoners and spoils of the enemy, and surrounded with the plaudits of rejoicing Rome. Paul looked little like such a hero: no car of victory carried him, he trode the causewayed road with wayworn foot; no medals or ornaments adorned his person, a chain or iron dangled from his wrist; no applauding crowds welcomed his approach, a few humble friends formed all his escort; yet never did a more truly conquering footstep fall on the pavement of Rome or *a heart more confident of victory pass within her gates.*[2]

3) Read Isaiah 6:9-10 in the context of Isaiah's call to appreciate Paul's quoting it in Acts 28:25-27.

ANALYSIS (28:14b-31)

1) This last segment of Acts is a passage that contains many items which appropriately conclude Luke's story. Divide the segment into the five paragraphs shown. When you begin to read the passage, concentrate on the first statement "and thus we came to Rome," recalling all the experiences of the sea journey which Luke had in mind when he wrote the word "thus." Now follow the established pattern of reading through the entire segment a few times, making notations in your Bible and on paper as you read.

2) Proceed with your observations and recordings on the analytical chart. Appropriately enough, the last word of Luke's

[2]James Stalker, *The Life of St. Paul* (New York: Fleming H. Revell Co., 1912), p. 134 (italics mine).

Acts 28:14b-31

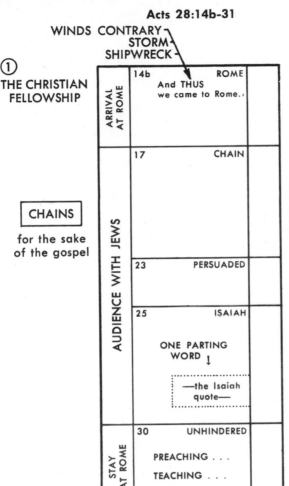

1. In each of the three middle paragraphs Paul is explaining a different subject. Record this in the right-hand narrow column. Use the other two
spaces for a related study.
2. Compare the first and last paragraphs with respect to Paul's situation.
3. Observe the two references to "kingdom of God." In both cases, what is
the context that immediately follows?
4. Make a consecutive study of the ministry of the gospel, beginning with
"Chains for the sake of the gospel," as shown.
5. Observe the different references to Jews in the paragraphs. Also, note
references to God.

narrative is the word translated "unhindered." One interesting study to make in this segment is to note the last major items recorded in Acts. You should find at least one in each paragraph. For example, the last reference to Christian fellowship is in the first paragraph. Record this study.

3) Observe that the three middle paragraphs describe Paul's audience with the Jews of Rome in some detail. How do the first and last paragraphs serve as introductory and concluding paragraphs, respectively?

4) The suggested studies given below the chart on page 235 will lead you into further channels of inquiry. (Having come to the end of your analytical study of the book of Acts, you have seen something of the large variety of studies that the Bible affords. One of the main purposes of this manual has been to suggest the unlimited number of study projects which the biblical text invites.)

5) Study the context of Paul's words, "For I am wearing this chain *for the sake of the hope of Israel.*" What did Paul mean by the last part of this statement?

6) What is the difference between seeing and perceiving (28:26)?

7) What do you learn from the small word "lest" in this quote: "And they have closed their eyes; lest they should see with their eyes, . . ." (28:27)?

8) In what way is the last paragraph of Acts (verses 30-31) a fitting climax to the entire book? How do the paragraphs about the Jews also figure prominently as a part of Acts' conclusion? In your own words, state the twofold conclusion of the book of Acts.

9) Acts does not record Paul's appearance before Nero (if he ever was brought before the emperor), nor the last months or years of the apostle's life. Does this detract from the purpose of Acts? How does the omission bolster the large theme of the book?

10) As you conclude this part of your study, write out some of the main spiritual lessons taught by the passage, concerning such subjects as Christian service, the gospel, perseverance, suffering.

EXPLANATIONS

1) "Accompanied by Aristarchus" (27:2). Paul called this friend his "fellow prisoner" in Colossians 4:10. Aristarchus was a faithful traveling companion on Paul's missionary journeys (Acts 19:29; 20:4), and now served with Luke as one of Paul's attendants.

2) "The brethren" (28:15). It is not known when or how the fellowship of Christians at Rome came into being. The "visitors from Rome" (2:10) who heard and responded to the gospel preached in Jerusalem on Pentecost Day may have been the seed of the new Christian community. By the time Paul wrote the epistle of Romans from the city of Corinth on his third missionary journey (A.D. 57), the church at Rome had matured measurably, the faith of its saints known "throughout the whole world" (Rom. 1:8). Paul's goal to reach Rome was not for the purpose of taking the gospel there for the first time. It was to give him opportunity to meet these new friends face to face, and as an apostolic representative of the church at large to officially identify the church as having reached the imperial city with the gospel.

3) "When we entered Rome" (28:16). This is the last "we" of Acts. But Luke obviously remained with Paul in Rome, for he appears in letters which Paul wrote from Rome (Philemon 24; Col. 4:14).

4) "With all openness" (28:31). The Greek word *parrēsiás* appears often in the New Testament, with these meanings:

  a) openly (that is, not secretly), "no one was speaking openly of Him" (John 7:13)

  b) plainly (clearly), "now You are speaking plainly" John 16:29

  c) with boldness, confidence, "we have confidence to enter the holy place" Hebrews 10:19

  It would appear that the first and third meanings correctly serve Luke's description of Paul's ministry at Rome.

5) "Unhindered" (28:31). This is the negative counterpart of the words just preceding it. As Luke watched the ink dry on the last word he wrote—*akōlútōs*, "unhindered"—the glow of it all must have stirred his heart to heights of gratitude to God. There

might have flashed before Luke's mind the countless attacks of
the last thirty years made by Satan's forces against the ministers
of God and the gospel they taught. In every instance God was
the victor. Some of His servants gave their lives, but the gospel
did not die. And now even Paul, though a prisoner of the state,
could preach and teach "concerning the Lord Jesus Christ with
all openness, *unhindered*"!

FURTHER ADVANCED STUDY

1) Paul probably wrote Colossians, Ephesians, Philemon and
Philippians[3] during this Roman imprisonment. The first three
were written at the same time, while Philippians was probably
written toward the end of his prison stay. Read these epistles
to ascertain what light they shed on his prison experience. Among
other things, observe the names of those who visited Paul at this
time. What was Paul's relationship to the church at Rome during
this period?

2) The New Testament affords little light on the origin of the
church at Rome. Philip Schaff writes, "The precise origin of the
church of Rome is involved in impenetrable mystery."[4] The first
Christian residents of Rome may have become believers (1)
through the ministry of Jesus in Palestine, (2) in connection with
the Holy Spirit's ministry on Pentecost Day,[5] (3) through the
ministry of believers scattered throughout different parts of the
empire because of persecution, or (4) through the ministry of
some of Paul's converts, such as Aquila and Priscilla. Inquire
further into this subject, seeking answers to such questions as:
What was the extent of the organization of the church at Rome
when Paul wrote Romans, and when he later arrived at Rome?

[3]The order listed here is that suggested by Merrill C. Tenney, *New Testament Survey* (Rev. ed.; Grand Rapids: Wm. B. Eerdmans Publishing Co.,
1961), p. 128.
[4]Philip Schaff, *Apostolic Christianity*, Vol. I, "History of the Christian
Church" (Grand Rapids: Wm. B. Eerdmans Publishing Co., 1952), p. 366.
[5]Of this Schaff writes, "In this case Peter, the preacher of the pentecostal
sermon, may be said to have had an *indirect* agency in the founding of the
church of Rome, which claims him as the rock on which it is built, although
the tradition of his early visit (42) and twenty or twenty-five years' residence
there is a long-exploded fable." *Ibid.*, p. 367.

What was Paul's personal relationship to this group of believers during his first stay in Rome under guard?[6]

3) Because of a minimum of explicit references to Paul's later life as contained in his epistles, there are differences of opinion over some subjects. For example, some New Testament scholars maintain that this imprisonment at Rome was Paul's last. Also, some believe such epistles as Philippians were written earlier in Paul's life, possibly during another imprisonment. You may want to refer to different books on Paul's life to become acquainted with these various views. (The position of this manual is given on pages 244-45.)

WORDS TO PONDER
"He . . . was welcoming all who came to him" (28:30).

---

[6]Your outside reading might include Schaff, *op. cit.*, pp. 360-75; and Frank J. Goodwin, *A Harmony of the Life of St. Paul* (3d ed.; New York: American Tract Socieyt, n.d.), pp. 220-21.

Part Four

CONCLUSION

A CONCLUDING STUDY IN ACTS

WE HAVE COME to the end of our study of the book of Acts. If we have opened our hearts to the teaching ministry of the Holy Spirit, we may confidently expect that the fruits of our study should continue to manifest themselves in at least these four ways:

1) Recall: The facts and lessons of Acts are "on call" in our hearts and minds, available for whatever situation may arise.

2) Return: No study of a book of the Bible should be considered the last one. We should have our appetite whetted to return for more.

3) Relationship: As we studied the story of the witnesses of Christ, we made personal decisions concerning our own relationship to Christ and His mission field. This should be a constantly growing relationship.

4) Relevance: As citizens of this contemporary world, our ears and eyes are alert to the times; Acts serves as one of our interpreters because of its relevance.

With the above things in mind, begin the summary suggested below as the last study project of this manual.

I. SUMMARY

A study of the different parts of Acts would not be complete without returning to the book as a whole to bring those parts together in a concise summary of Luke's theme.

We have seen that Luke's starting point was in the word "witness," as spoken by Jesus to His apostles. So it was Luke's task to write the story of the witness of various people of God for the first thirty years after Christ's ascension. Interwoven throughout the action-packed record are various aspects of that witness. As your concluding study, summarize what Acts presents on the following subjects:

> 1) Word of the witness
> 2) Workers of the witness
> 3) Work of the witness
> 4) Fruits of the witness

You should be able to write at least ten concise statements for each of the four categories. Let your statements be broad, yet explicit enough to include the primary truths of Acts (e.g., under workers, do not merely list the names of ten men).

II. EVENTS IN PAUL'S LIFE AFTER ACTS

Acts does not relate the last of Paul's life. Tradition plus statements made by Paul in letters written after his first imprisonment furnish this story:

A. *Release* (A.D. 62)

Paul was either acquitted in his trial before Nero, or the trial never commenced for want of a case against the apostle. That Paul was confident of being released is evident from Philemon 22. (Cf. Phil. 1:25).

B. *Period of liberty* (A.D. 62-66)

1. Travels. Paul's itinerary is unknown, but it probably included such places as Spain, northern Greece and Macedonia, Crete, Ephesus and Troas, possibly in that order.

2. Writings. Paul's first letter to Timothy was written from Macedonia, A.D. 66. Paul's letter to Titus was written from Ephesus, A.D. 66.

3. Arrest. The burning of Rome (A.D. 64) was attributed to Christians by Nero, and a violent persecution broke out. Among others, Paul was a marked man. Stalker writes, "Every Roman governor knew that he could not do the emperor a more pleasing

service than by sending to him Paul in chains."[1] His arrest took place A.D. 66 or 67.

C. *Second imprisonment* (A.D. 67)[2]

In this imprisonment, Paul was treated as the worst of criminals. From prison he was able to write another letter to his co-laborer, the epistle now known as II Timothy. It is Paul's dying letter and reveals much of the triumphant spirit of the apostle who knew his course was finished. If he was granted a trial, justice was not invited to the courtroom. Stalker writes of this, "On the judgment-seat, clad in the imperial purple, sat a man who in a bad world had attained the eminence of being the very worst and meanest being in it. . . . and in the prisoner's dock stood the best man the world contained, his hair whitened with labors for the good of men and the glory of God."[3]

D. *Death* (A.D. 67)

Nero's verdict was "guilty." According to tradition, Paul was executed by the headsman's ax.

III. EVENTS IN PETER'S LIFE AFTER ACTS

The last reference to Peter in Acts is in chapter 15 at the Jerusalem council. It is very easy, therefore, for the reader of Acts to miss the fact that Peter's vital ministry of the gospel did not cease then. While Paul was traveling on his evangelistic crusades, Peter also was preaching in various provinces of the Mediterranean world. Peter's salutation in his first epistle is addressed to believers scattered throughout Pontus, Galatia, Cappadocia, Asia and Bithynia. Of Peter's relationship to the churches in these areas, Tenney writes, "While there is no statement on record that Peter founded or even visited these churches, there is nothing to preclude his doing so."[4]

[1]Philip Schaff, *Apostolic Christianity*, Vol. I, "History of the Christian Church" (Grand Rapids: Wm. B. Eerdmans Publishing Co., 1952), p. 141.
[2]See Schaff, *op. cit.*, pages 331-33, for a brief discussion of the question of Paul's second Roman captivity. For the arguments in favor of the two-captivity view, read Frank J. Goodwin, *A Harmony of the Life of St. Paul* (3d ed.; New York: American Tract Society, n.d.), pp. 215-20.
[3]James Stalker, *The Life of St. Paul* (Rev. ed.; New York: Fleming H. Revell Co., 1912), p. 143.
[4]Merrill C. Tenney, *New Testament Survey* (Rev. ed.; Grand Rapids: Wm. B. Eerdmans Publishing Co., 1961), p. 345.

Peter was not the founder of the church at Rome nor its leader,[5] though it is generally believed that he spent a short time in the city soon after Paul's liberation and toward the end of his life. His two epistles were written about this time, with an interval between them. At the time of his second letter he knew his death was imminent (II Peter 1:14). According to tradition his death was by crucifixion head-downward at the hands of Nero, about the same time his "beloved brother Paul" (II Peter 3:15) also was martyred. Of this Rackham writes, "So the two protagonists of the church, the apostle of the circumcision and the apostle of the uncircumcision, were united in death . . . . But if Rome triumphed over S. Peter and S. Paul, their deaths presaged the downfall of the heathen city, and their tombs were to become the glory of the Christian city."[6]

IV. CONCLUSION

At the beginning of our study we observed that Luke wrote two different accounts centered about Christ to give this grand twofold story of the gospel:

1) The facts of the gospel. "All that Jesus began to do and teach" (Acts 1:1). Luke told this story in his gospel.

2) The work of the gospel. "Orders to the apostles" (Acts 1:2). Luke told this story in his Acts.

For twenty centuries now God has not been without loyal witnesses, compelled by fire in their bones to share the glad tidings of Jesus with all the world. May it be the earnest desire of our hearts to be counted among such a number.

A noble army, men and boys, the matron and the maid,
Around the Saviour's throne rejoice, in robes of light arrayed:
They climbed the steep ascent of heaven through peril, toil and pain:
O God, to us may grace be given to follow in their train.

—REGINALD HEBER

[5]If Peter was an active leader in the church at Rome when Paul arrived in the city, Luke's account would surely have made a point of this, since Peter is the main character in the first half of Luke's narrative. (See Richard B. Rackham, *The Acts of the Apostles* (13th ed.; London: Methuen & Co., Ltd., 1947), pp. 509-10 for a further discussion of this.)
[6]Rackham, *op. cit.*, p. 512.

APPENDIX

RULERS DURING THE TIMES OF ACTS

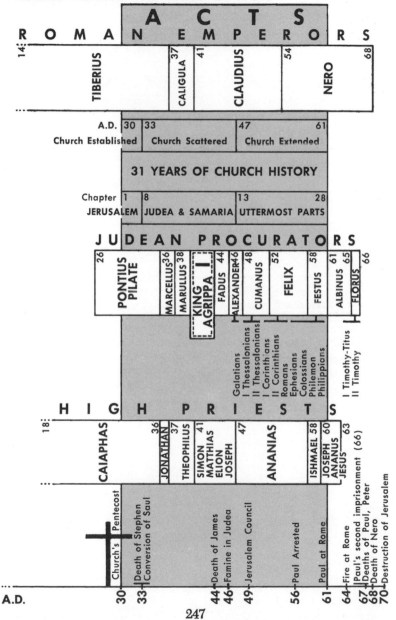

ACTS

ROMAN EMPERORS

14; TIBERIUS | CALIGULA 37 | 41 CLAUDIUS 54 | NERO 68

A.D. 30 Church Established | 33 Church Scattered | 47 Church Extended | 61

31 YEARS OF CHURCH HISTORY

Chapter 1 JERUSALEM | 8 JUDEA & SAMARIA | 13 UTTERMOST PARTS | 28

JUDEAN PROCURATORS

26 PONTIUS PILATE | MARCELLUS 36 | MARULLUS 38 | KING AGRIPPA I | FADUS 44 | ALEXANDER 46 | CUMANUS 48 | FELIX 52 | FESTUS 58 | ALBINUS 61 | FLORUS 65 | 66

Galatians
I Thessalonians
II Thessalonians
I Corinthians
II Corinthians
Romans
Ephesians
Colossians
Philemon
Philippians

I Timothy-Titus
II Timothy

HIGH PRIESTS

18; CAIAPHAS | JONATHAN 36 | THEOPHILUS 37 | SIMON 41 | MATTHIAS | ELION | JOSEPH 47 | ANANIAS | ISHMAEL 58 | JOSEPH 60 | ANANUS | JESUS 63

Church's Pentecost
Death of Stephen
Conversion of Saul
Death of James
Famine in Judea
Jerusalem Council
Paul Arrested
Paul at Rome
Fire at Rome
Paul's second imprisonment (66)
Deaths of Paul, Peter
Death of Nero
Destruction of Jerusalem

A.D. 30 33 44 46 49 56 61 64 67 68 70

247

BIBLIOGRAPHY

I. *Books cited in the footnotes, and other recommended volumes*

Atlas of the Bible Lands. Maplewood, N.J.: C. S. Hammond & Co., 1954.

BLAIKLOCK, E. M. *The Acts of the Apostles.* Grand Rapids: Wm. B Eerdmans Publishing Co., 1959. A brief commentary, but very readable.

BOYER, JAMES L. *New Testament Chronological Chart.* Revised edition. Winona Lake, Ind.: Grace Theological Seminary, 1962. This very valuable tool for New Testament study gives the chronology of the ministries of Jesus and the apostles and shows the contemporaneous historical items of the extrabiblical scene of the first century.

BROWN, CHARLES. *The Acts of the Apostles.* 2 vols. London: The Religious Tract Society, n.d.

BRUCE, F. F. *The Acts of the Apostles.* Chicago: Inter-Varsity Press, 1952. This book was written mainly for the Greek student. Most of the commentary section is included in Bruce's later work, *Commentary on the Book of Acts.*

———. *Commentary on the Book of Acts.* Grand Rapids: Wm. B. Eerdmans Publishing Co., 1954. This is one of the best commentaries on Acts available today.

———. *Israel and the Nations.* Grand Rapids: Wm. B. Eerdmans Publishing Co., 1963.

———. *The Letters of Paul: an Expanded Paraphrase.* Grand Rapids: Wm. B. Eerdmans Publishing Co., 1965.

CARTER, CHARLES W. and EARLE, RALPH. *The Acts of the Apostles.* Grand Rapids: Zondervan Publishing House, 1959.

CLARK, GEO. W. *The Acts of the Apostles.* Revised edition. Philadelphia: The American Baptist Publication Society, 1896.

CONYBEARE, W. J. and HOWSON, J. S. *The Life and Epistles of St. Paul.* Grand Rapids: Wm. B. Eerdmans Publishing Co., 1950. This is considered a standard work on the life of Paul.

DANA, H. E. *The New Testament World.* Revised edition. Nashville: Broadman Press, 1937.

DAVIDSON, F. (ed.). *The New Bible Commentary.* Grand Rapids: Wm. B. Eerdmans Publishing Co., 1963.

DAVIS, JOHN D. *The Westminster Dictionary of the Bible.* Revised edition. Philadelphia: The Westminster Press, 1944.

DOUGLAS, J. D. (ed.). *The New Bible Dictionary.* Grand Rapids: Wm. B. Eerdmans Publishing Co., 1962. A valuable, up-to-date Bible dictionary.

ELLIS, E. EARLE. *Paul and His Recent Interpreters.* Grand Rapids: Wm. B. Eerdmans Publishing Co., 1961.

FARRAR, F. W. *The Life and Work of St. Paul.* New York: E. P. Dutton & Co., 1893.

FINEGAN, JACK. *Light from the Ancient Past.* Princeton: Princeton University Press, 1946.

GETTYS, JOSEPH M. *How to Study Acts.* Richmond: John Knox Press, 1959.

GOODWIN, FRANK J. *A Harmony of the Life of St. Paul.* (3rd ed.) New York: American Tract Society, n.d. A valuable tool for the student of the life of Paul. All parts of the New Testament that have any relation to Paul's life, including his actual writing of the epistles, are woven into a continuous chronology.

HASTINGS, JAMES. (ed.). *Dictionary of the Bible.* Revised edition. FREDERICK C. GRANT and H. H. ROWLEY. (eds.). New York: Charles Scribner's Sons, 1963.

The International Standard Bible Encyclopaedia. ORR, JAMES. (ed.). 5 vols. Grand Rapids: Wm. B. Eerdmans Publishing Co., 1952.

JENSEN, IRVING L. *Independent Bible Study.* Chicago: Moody Press, 1963.

LANGE, JOHN PETER. *Commentary on the Holy Scriptures: Acts.* Grand Rapids: Zondervan Publishing House. Reprint edition, n.d.

LATOURETTE, KENNETH SCOTT. *A History of the Expansion of Christianity.* Vol. I. New York: Harper & Bros., 1937.

LIGHTFOOT, J. B. *St. Paul's Epistle to the Galatians.* London: Macmillan & Co., 1890.

LONGENECKER, RICHARD N. *Paul, Apostle of Liberty.* New York: Harper & Row, Publishers, Inc., 1964.

MANLEY, O. T. (ed.). *The New Bible Handbook.* Chicago: Inter-Varsity Press, 1963.

MORGAN, G. CAMPBELL. *The Acts of the Apostles.* New York: Fleming H. Revell Co., 1924.

PFEIFFER, CHARLES F., and HARRISON, EVERETT F. (eds.). *The Wycliffe Bible Commentary.* Chicago: Moody Press, 1962.

PFEIFFER, CHARLES F., and VOS, HOWARD F. *The Wycliffe Historical Geography of Bible Lands.* Chicago: Moody Press, 1967.

PHILLIPS, J. B. *New Testament in Modern English.* New York: The Macmillan Co., 1958.

PURVES, GEORGE T. *Christianity in the Apostolic Age.* New York: Charles Scribner's Sons, 1929.

RACKHAM, RICHARD B. *The Acts of the Apostles*. (13th ed.). London: Methuen and Co., Ltd., 1947. This comprehensive commentary was first published in 1901. It is one of the best works on Acts.

RAMSAY, W. M. *The Cities of St. Paul*. New York: George H. Doran Co., n.d.

———. *Luke the Physician*. Grand Rapids: Baker Book House, 1956.

———. *Pictures of the Apostolic Church*. Philadelphia: The Sunday School Times Co., 1910.

———. *St. Paul the Traveler*. Grand Rapids: Baker Book House, 1951.

ROBERTSON, A. T. *Epochs in the Life of Paul*. New York: Charles Scribner's Sons, 1923.

———. *Word Pictures in the New Testament* Vol. III. New York: Harper & Bros., 1930.

SALMON, EDWARD T. *A History of the Roman World from 30 B.C. to A.D. 138*. New York: The Macmillan Co., 1944.

SAUER, ERICH. *The Dawn of World Redemption*. Grand Rapids: Wm. B. Eerdmans Publishing Co., 1953.

SCHAFF, PHILIP. "History of the Christian Church." Vol. I: *Apostolic Christianity*. Grand Rapids: Wm. B. Eerdmans Publishing Co., 1952.

SCROGGIE, W. GRAHAM. *Know Your Bible*. Vol. II. London: Pickering & Inglis Ltd., n.d.

STALKER, JAMES. *The Life of St. Paul*. Revised edition. New York: Fleming H. Revell Co., 1912.

STIFLER, J. M. *An Introduction to the Study of the Acts of the Apostles*. New York: Fleming H. Revell Co., 1892.

STRONG, JAMES. *The Exhaustive Concordance of the Bible*. New York: Abingdon-Cokesbury Press, 1947.

TENNEY, MERRILL C. *New Testament Survey*. Revised edition. Grand Rapids: Wm. B. Eerdmans Publishing Co., 1961. One of the best books written in the field of New Testament survey.

———. *New Testament Times*. Grand Rapids: Wm. B. Eerdmans Publishing Co., 1965.

THOMAS, W. H. GRIFFITH. *Outline Studies in Acts*. Grand Rapids: Wm. B. Eerdmans Publishing Co., 1956.

TRENCH, RICHARD C. *Synonyms of the New Testament*. Grand Rapids: Wm. B. Eerdmans Publishing Co., 1948.

VINCENT, MARVIN R. *Word Studies in the New Testament*, Vol. I. Grand Rapids: Wm. B. Eerdmans Publishing Co., 1946.

WALKER, THOMAS. *The Acts of the Apostles*. Chicago: Moody Press. Reprint edition, 1965.

WALVOORD, JOHN F. *The Holy Spirit*. Wheaton, Ill.: Van Kampen Press, 1954.

WRIGHT, GEORGE E., and FILSON, FLOYD V. *The Westminster Historical Atlas to the Bible*. Philadelphia: The Westminster Press, 1946.

WUEST, KENNETH S. *The New Testament: An Expanded Translation.* Grand Rapids: Wm. B. Eerdmans Publishing Co., 1961.
YOUNG, ROBERT. *Analytical Concordance to the Bible.* Grand Rapids: Wm. B. Eerdmans Publishing Co., 1951.

II. Books listed in "Further Advanced Study" sections

ALLEN, ROLAND. *Missionary Methods: St. Paul's or Ours.* Grand Rapids: Wm. B. Eerdmans Publishing Co., 1962.
ALLIS, OSWALD T. *Prophecy and the Church.* Philadelphia: The Presbyterian and Reformed Publishing Co., 1945.
BARNHOUSE, DONALD GREY. *The Invisible War.* Grand Rapids: Zondervan Publishing Co., 1965.
BERKOUWER, G. C. *Faith and Sanctification.* Grand Rapids: Wm. B. Eerdmans Publishing Co., 1952.
BOUNDS, EDWARD M. *Satan.* Grand Rapids: Baker Book House, 1963.
BRISCOE, D. STUART. *The Fullness of Christ.* Grand Rapids: Zondervan Publishing House, 1965.
BROOMALL, WICK. *The Holy Spirit.* Grand Rapids: Baker Book House, 1963.
BUIS, HARRY. *The Doctrine of Eternal Punishment.* Philadelphia: The Presbyterian and Reformed Publishing Co., 1957.
BUNYAN, JOHN. *The Holy War.* Chicago: Moody Press. Reprint edition, 1948.
CHAFER, LEWIS SPERRY. *He That Is Spiritual.* Wheaton, Ill.: Van Kampen Press, 1918.
———. *The Kingdom in History and Prophecy.* Findlay, Ohio: Dunham Publishing Co., 1915.
———. *Satan.* Philadelphia: The Sunday School Times Co., 1922.
DOWNEY, MURRAY W. *The Art of Soul Winning.* Grand Rapids: Baker Book House, 1957.
EDERSHEIM, A. *Sketches of Jewish Social Life.* Grand Rapids: Wm. B. Eerdmans Publishing Co., 1950.
———. *The Temple: Its Ministry and Services.* Revised edition. Grand Rapids: Wm. B. Eerdmans Publishing Co., 1950.
EVANS, WILLIAM. *Personal Soul-Winning.* Chicago: Moody Press, 1948.
FERM, ROBERT O. *The Psychology of Christian Conversion.* New York: Fleming H. Revell Co., 1959.
GORDON, S. D. *Quiet Talks About the Tempter.* New York: Fleming H. Revell Co., 1910.
GRAY, JAMES M. *Spiritism and the Fallen Angels.* New York: Fleming H. Revell Co., 1920.
HALLESBY, O. *Conscience.* Minneapolis: Augsburg Publishing House, 1933.

IRONSIDE, H. A. *Holiness—The False and the True.* London: Pickering & Inglis, Ltd. 1935.

KOCH, KURT E. *Between Christ and Satan.* Grand Rapids: Kregel Publications, 1961.

KRUMMACHER, F. W. *The Suffering Saviour.* Chicago: Moody Press, 1947.

KUIPER, R. B. *God-Centered Evangelism.* Grand Rapids: Baker Book House, 1961.

KUYPER, ABRAHAM. *The Work of the Holy Spirit.* Grand Rapids: Wm. B. Eerdmans Publishing Co., 1941.

LADD, GEORGE E. *The Blessed Hope.* Grand Rapids: Wm. B. Eerdmans Publishing Co., 1956.

———. *Jesus and the Kingdom.* New York: Harper & Row Publishers, Inc., 1964.

LAIDLAW, JOHN. *Miracles of Our Lord.* Grand Rapids: Baker Book House, 1956.

LEWIS, C. S. *Miracles.* New York: The Macmillan Co., 1947.

———. *The Problem of Pain.* New York: The Macmillan Co., 1944.

MACAULAY, J. C., and BELTON, ROBERT H. *Personal Evangelism.* Chicago: Moody Press, 1960.

MAXWELL, L. E. *Born Crucified.* Chicago: Moody Press, 1945.

McCLAIN, ALVA J. *The Greatness of the Kingdom.* Chicago: Moody Press, 1959.

MORRIS, LEON. *The Biblical Doctrine of Judgment.* Grand Rapids: Wm. B. Eerdmans Publishing Co., 1960.

———. *The Spirit of the Living God.* Chicago: Inter-Varsity Press, 1960.

NEE, WATCHMAN. *The Normal Christian Life.* Revised edition. Fort Washington, Pa.: Christian Literature Crusade, 1962.

NEVIUS, JOHN L. *Demon Possession and Allied Themes.* New York: Fleming H. Revell Co., n.d.

OLFORD, STEPHEN. *The Secret of Soul-Winning.* Chicago: Moody Press, 1963.

OWEN, JOHN. *The Holy Spirit: His Gifts and Power.* Grand Rapids: Kregel Publications, 1961.

PACHE, RENE. *The Future Life.* Chicago: Moody Press, 1962.

———. *The Person and Work of the Holy Spirit.* Chicago: Moody Press, 1954.

PAXSON, RUTH. *Life on the Highest Plane.* Chicago: Moody Press, 1928.

PENTECOST, J. DWIGHT. *Prophecy for Today.* Grand Rapids: Zondervan Publishing House, 1961.

PETERS, GEORGE N. H. *Theocratic Kingdom.* 3 vols. Grand Rapids: Kregel Publications, 1957.

RAMM, BERNARD. *The Witness of the Spirit.* Grand Rapids: Wm. B. Eerdmans Publishing Co., 1960.

REHWINKEL, ALFRED M. *The Voice of Conscience.* St. Louis: Concordia Publishing House, 1956.

RYLE, J. C. *Holiness.* Grand Rapids: Kregel Publications, 1962.

RYRIE, CHARLES C. *The Basis of the Premillennial Faith.* Neptune, N.J.: Loizeaux Brothers Inc., 1953.

SAUER, ERICH. *In the Arena of Faith.* Grand Rapids: Wm. B. Eerdmans Publishing Co., 1955.

SCHILDER, KLAAS. *Christ in His Suffering.* Grand Rapids: Wm. B. Eerdmans Publishing Co., 1958.

SEAMANDS, JOHN T. *The Supreme Task of the Church.* Grand Rapids: Wm. B. Eerdmans Publishing Co., 1964.

SMITH, ARTHUR E. *The Temple and Its Teaching.* Chicago: Moody Press, 1956.

SMITH, J. WILBUR. *Therefore, Stand.* Chicago: Moody Press, 1945.

SPURGEON, CHARLES HADDON. *The Soul-Winner.* Grand Rapids: Wm. B. Eerdmans Publishing Co., 1963.

SWETE, HENRY BARCLAY. *The Holy Spirit in the New Testament.* Grand Rapids: Baker Book House, 1964.

THIELICKE, HELMUT. *Between God and Satan.* Grand Rapids: Wm. B. Eerdmans Publishing Co., 1959.

THOMAS, W. H. GRIFFITH. *The Holy Spirit of God.* Chicago: Moody Press, 1913.

TORREY, REUBEN A. *The Holy Spirit.* New York: Fleming H. Revell Co., 1927.

———. *How to Work for Christ.* New York: Fleming H. Revell Co., 1901.

TOURNIER, PAUL. *Guilt and Grace.* New York: Harper & Bros., 1962.

TRENCH, RICHARD C. *Notes on the Miracles of Our Lord.* London: Society for Promoting Christian Knowledge, 1904.

UNGER, MERRILL F. *Biblical Demonology.* Wheaton, Ill.: Van Kampen Press, 1952.

WALLACE, RONALD S. *The Gospel Miracles.* Grand Rapids: Wm. B. Eerdmans Publishing Co., 1960.

WALVOORD, JOHN F. *The Church in Prophecy.* Grand Rapids: Zondervan Publishing House, 1964.

———. *The Holy Spirit.* Wheaton, Ill.: Van Kampen Press, 1954.

———. *The Millennial Kingdom.* Findlay, Ohio: Dunham Publishing Co., 1959.